OPTIONS

TRADING

A simple way for everyone to do business.

What if this book could show you an easy way to make
money? Make a passive income with new techniques.

J.MARK CLARK

TABLE OF CONTENTS

Introduction

Welcome to Options Trading: A Simple Way for All Ages to Do Business; What If This Book Could Show You an Easy Way to Make Money? Make A Passive Income with New Techniques. In this book, we'll introduce you to the exciting and challenging world of options. Some of the topics we'll be discussing in this book include:

- Learning what options are and how to make money through it

- Find out the risks of not investing

- Answer the question: how to maximize profits?

- Learn to avoid common trading errors and mistakes.

- Find out how to choose right trading strategies

And much more!

Options' trading is not for everyone. Before you jump in, you should study options carefully, so you know what you're getting into.

- Understand your risk profile: If you are not a risk taker and see bonds and mutual funds as places where you want to put your money, options might be too risky for you. However, you should learn about them first. There are several options when it comes to options that can help reduce risk, so there may be a place for you in the space. It is best to learn it firsthand to get a better idea of what your profile is and how you prefer to trade.

- Understand your financial situation: Before jumping into any new investment program, make sure you have a clear picture of where you stand financially. You should know where you are at for income, credit card debts, taxes, other loans, and obligations. Have a clear idea of how much capital you can really afford to lose.

- Be an analyst, not a careless risk taker: Options require a deeper understanding of the markets than regular stock trading does. The excitement that arises from the possibility of fast and large profits can overwhelm some people, leading to excessive risk-taking. Be aware of this and put the time in to do analysis rather than looking only for a fast buck.

Being successful in trading requires hard work and a lot of studying, and this concept applies not only to option trading but also to all financial actions of this kind. Be mindful about time scales in options trading and remember that in the first few days or a few weeks you won't see any dramatic shifts in the value of your options. The reason for this is the fact that the trading profit actually comes from the loss of other traders. The way of getting profit is the same whether you trade derivatives, shares or options. The amount of money that goes around is smaller when you reduce the commissions that dealers and brokers take. These amounts of money are one of the reasons why many traders lose during the trade. You should educate yourself to avoid the fate of most of these brokers. Learn how to trade more smartly, as it will help you thrive or, at worst, to survive in the trading market. Consider these next pages simply as a start of your options trading journey in which you will be able to recognize and define the basic terms and strategies for your future career. It should give you the grounding that you need and motivate you to search forward and educate yourself further.

All trading and investment activity carry with it some risk. If done correctly, a trader can earn substantial profits from their activities; however, some traders will be at risk of losing substantial amounts of money. No guarantees can be made, and the topics discussed in this book are presented for informational and educational purposes only and are not to be taken as actual financial advice. The best teacher yet experiences and once you know the basics, it is time to get your feet wet and apply what you have learned!

CHAPTER 1:

Step Guide on How to Make Money with Option

One can gain a real advantage in the market if one knows how options work and can use them properly since you can put the cards in your favor if you can use options correctly. The great thing about options is that you can use them according to your style. A lot of Multi-National Corporations (MNCs) use options in many ways. Some companies may give employees potential stock ownership as stock options or use options to hedge foreign-exchange risk.

Getting It All Started

You may be excited to jump into the market and start trading right away, but there are a few things that you will need to do first. You will need to start out with a good understanding of the basics that come with options and you need to know some of the option types that you can pick from. We talked about these topics a little bit before, but the more that you can learn about them before investing, the more success you will have.

After you have had some time to understand what options all are about and what you will be getting yourself into, it is time to come up with your motivation for trading. Ask yourself how much money you are looking to make from this trade and how you would like to use that money when you have earned it. This motivation is going to help you out so much when you are in the thick of the trading and you need some help staying focus.

But one of the most important things that you will need to focus on when you first get started is having what is called a trading plan. The trading plan is going to basically list all of the things that you want to be able to accomplish while you are trading.

It can include what you expect to happen, some of your goals, the strategy that you will go with, and any other guidelines that will help you be successful.

Those who decide to start investing in options without having a good plan in place will be the ones who run into a lot of risks.

Determine Whether You Will Proceed as A Company or An Individual

Both these alternatives are a lot different when actual options trading come into practice. The legal obligations of both vary significantly. Besides, check whether you're allowed to trade with an offshore company or an offshore bank account. This could be advantageous in some tax-related situations. Non-resident citizen offshore companies and bank accounts are quite beneficial.

Get A Trading Account

Setting up an online trading account is the foremost thing to do when starting trading in options. Step by step instructions is provided by companies, which makes it very easy to manage the account. But this process does take some time, so start early. A lot of factors are taken into consideration while deciding on your trading account.

The amount of money you're planning to invest in is the first thing that defines the type of account, which will be opened. A very modest amount of start-up money is required to start trading in stock only. Even 200$ will work. However, a Basic options account requires a minimum start-up of 2000$. If you have enough capital, setting up a day-trading account shall be an optimal choice. This account enables you to buy and sell as many times as you want.

After selling a stock or option, you get the money immediately, which in turn enables you to buy again. Some time is required in a regular account to clear the proceeds from a sale. A Margin Account enables you to borrow money to trade while using your own capital at the same time. One can say that it is similar to an overdraft facility, which allows you to get extra funds.

There's a catch though: a margin account requires a lot of time to be approved. You can start with a regular account and apply for a margin account eventually. You must use your own money in a regular account and setting it up is less time-consuming.

The Need for Research Companies and Their Relevance

Acquiring the best research information can be a tedious task. The market has a lot of research groups. To make successful trades and make your ventures profitable, up to date information about options is of utmost importance. One needs to be completely aware of the existing market conditions. So, you can look for companies that provide this information and make more informed decisions.

Select a Security

This can be done by researching the finance segments of major news corporations. A simple search will turn up results such as CNN's Money segment, which lists the most active companies according to the S&P 500. If the investor is already partially immersed in the finance world, it would be wise to seek out the advice of a friend or mentor. New options traders, and particularly those who are new to trading in general, should approach options trading cautiously. Rather than diving right in, investors should get their feet wet by experimenting with a limited number of securities and options so that they can keep track of gains and losses and avoid mistakes for future investments.

Choose OTC or Regulated Trading

While this can be decided at another stage, it is suggested here so that new investors can refer to the boards of a regulated exchange, such as the New York Stock Exchange, when choosing a put or call that is well suited to their tastes. Practiced traders can pick up an OTC option if desired, such as a call to cover the cost of an insurance put, also known as a married put.

Select Strategies

Before beginning trading, investors will need to be sure they are familiar with a few simple strategies that can be implemented with a stock.

Examine the Market

Investors will need to study the time frame charts associated with their underlying security selection. Take into account all three trends in regard to the time frame and note how the security is moving within each.

Purchase Options and Trade

Finally, the moment investors have been waiting for. Based upon conclusions drawn from studying time frame charts, investors will need to buy the appropriate calls or puts. At the same time, investors should choose one or two of the strategies with which they are already familiar that they believe will work well in the present market climate. If trading via a regulated exchange, options for the strategies may be selected from a list published by the exchange.

Getting A Broker

Interactive Brokers are favorable in case you open only one account. They offer quick options information while being less expensive than other alternatives.

A lot of online brokers can be found, but they charge a certain amount for their services, which can affect your profit margin in the initial stages of trading.

The broker is going to be the person who works with you and often will be able to give you advice and help you to make the trades that you want. All brokers that you go with will require some fees or a commission that you will need to pay to use their services, so you must factor this in when figuring out the costs that you want to incur. There are many different types of brokers that you are able to go with and the price that you pay will depend on the type and amount of services you choose to go with.

When you pick out the broker you want to work with, you will probably need to meet with them in the beginning and discuss your trading plan and how they will be able to help. They will go over a risk assessment with you, so they know where you stand with the amount of risks that you are willing to take. It is a good place for you and the broker to get started together so you are on the same page and are able to get things done.

Appreciate That Options Trading Is Not Simple

It is vital at this stage to recapitulate the meaning of options trading. This is a contract that grants one the right of either buying or selling a security based on the speculative value of it in a limited period of time. However, the contract is not obligatory in nature. In understanding options trading, two forms of it have to be understood; first is a call option, and the other is the put option. The two are opposites of each other. One buys the former option when one expects an asset's value to go up over time but before the deadline of expiry of the contract expires.

However, participating in this market requires one to have enough understanding of how it works. Any venture requires one to learn enough. Educating oneself generally about investment is the best standing point. This creates understanding and ensures that one is able to comprehend the way that the options trading market as an investment venture works.

Among the reasons why people should educate themselves on options trading is because it does not work in certain ways. It also does not have guarantees of profit. This means that it, just like other ventures, involves risks that should be understood. The risks in the case of trading options are quite extreme. It requires calculation and being accurate as one speculates about the drop and rising of the value of the options on offer. Being interest in a venture that involves a high-risk level requires enough knowledge and sometimes mentorship by those who have prior knowledge and understanding of the market in order to avoid plunging into frustration and wastage of capital.

CHAPTER 2:

Investor Do's and Do Not's

What Every Investor Should Do?

<u>Understand Market Basics</u>

In the modern world, investment has been made accessible to the average person. Most employers who offer retirement savings plans often sponsor an education day, so employees can gain some familiarity with the types of retirement plans and options that are available to them. In addition, with the proliferation of cable news networks, specialized programming, the internet, and social media, there is no shortage of information widely available to virtually anyone, anywhere.

Especially in the today's information age, knowledge is power. Before you jump right into trading on the options market, take some time to familiarize yourself with the basics of market dynamics. Options traders use a technical language that is unique to their niche in the investment world, and many outsiders may be completely perplexed and unable to understand much of what they say. In addition, the ability to tolerate a certain amount of financial risk is an inseparable component of successful investing.

Play by the Rules

As an options trader, you will be in competition with other traders and investors. Much of your success in investing--including making valuable connections in the investment world--will result from your ability to play by the rules. The stock market is a living thing, and the activity of traders has a huge impact on its health and volatility. We are all tempted to be maverick investors who leave a legacy of innovation but understanding the fundamentals will work in your favor. Specifically, option prices increase or decrease as a result of changes in share prices and volatility. So, when share prices increase, call options make money and put options lose money; when share prices decrease, put options make money and call options lose money. Options also move in relation to volatility; when share prices are stable, greater volatility can increase the options pricing. So, when volatility increases, buying options makes money; when volatility decreases, selling options makes money.

Understanding these four basic rules can help you become a better trader.

Adapt Your Strategy to Market Conditions

Once you're up and running in the world of professional options trading, you will gain confidence as you see your efforts pay off in returns to your options account. As you move from a Level 1 trading account to a Level 2 trading account, you will likely develop a preference for a certain type of options trades—maybe covered calls or married puts. Familiarity with the language and mechanics of the options trading profession is definitely something that will work in your favor. However, it is important to remember that as you move up the ladder, you will gain access to a wider array of trading tools and strategies. As you gain knowledge and experience, remember that no matter how comfortable you have become with a select number of options trading strategies, there will always be additional aspects of nuance that can enhance your skill as a trader and increase the profitability of your efforts. The key to ensuring success is not just in choosing the best strategy in relation to the performance of the underlying asset. You must also consider the overall market conditions and whether those conditions may have an effect on the future performance of that asset. Although one strategy may have worked in the past under similar conditions, considering changes in current conditions will help you adjust your strategy to ensure you continue to build on your past success.

Always Have an Exit Plan

Picking a stock, formulating an options strategy to generate income from the stock's performance, and then contacting your broker to initiate an opening transaction is a good beginning. Nonetheless, this plan is not a complete strategy. The most important part of any options strategy is not how to get in—it's how to get out.

The payoff of an options strategy may result from buying the underlying stock at below market value, from accepting a cash settlement deposit for a put option on stock with declining value, or even from profiting from an increase in the cost of the options premium by selling the contract before it expires.

However, you believe the asset you have identified may provide you with an opportunity to construct a profitable options trading strategy, conjecture and hope should not be part of that strategy. Before you complete an opening transaction, make sure you are very clear about your specific goal for entering the contract. After you complete the opening transaction, you will be faced with one of three possible outcomes:

1. The market and the target stocks moved in the direction you predicted.

2. The market or the target stocks move in a direction you did not predict, resulting in unexpected losses.

3. The market or the target stocks move in a direction you did not predict, resulting in unexpected gains.

Similarly, you should have three responses ready for each of these developments:

1. If you are faced with the first result, you should have an exit strategy already prepared. Whatever else is happening around you, as long as your assets are on the right track, do not deviate from your plan.

2. If there are unexpected changes that are not favorable to your position on the underlying asset, what plan did you formulate to exit the contract so you can minimize your losses?

3. If there are unexpected changes that are favorable to your position on the underlying asset, what plan did you formulate to exit the contract so you can capitalize on these gains?

No matter what happens, make sure you can answer all 3 questions before you enter an options contract. Then, once you have laid the groundwork for a successful options trade, stick with your plan, even if you think you could make a few more dollars by improvising.

What Every Investor Should Avoid

<u>Doubling up to Cover Losses</u>

"Doubling up" is a prime example of how an options trader may ignore his original exit strategy if the market or the underlying stocks fail to perform the way he had expected when he originally constructed his strategy.

For example, let's say a trader buys a call option for 100 shares of Company B, with a strike price of $45. At the time he purchased the call option, Company B was trading at $44. The trader expects the share price to rise to $47 before the contract expires. Immediately after the opening transaction, though, the stock price slips to $43.

To compensate for any potential losses if the stock rises to only $46, the trader may be tempted to "double up" by buying another $45 call option at the reduced premium price.

If this trader were only purchasing stocks, he may have celebrated the unexpected drop in share value and immediately purchased as many additional shares as possible, with a goal of greater long-term return. But options trading works differently. The options trader is focused on short-term returns, and if the stock price fails to put the contract in-the-money by the expiration date, the trader loses on not only one contract, but two.

The smart trader will remember that he created an exit plan for this scenario and will stick with it. Though it may be tempting to purchase an additional call option, he should judge the wisdom of such a purchase by asking himself if he would buy the second call option if he were not already in the middle of a trade. If this is not ordinarily a contract he would enter into--and it isn't, because that was definitely not his strategy in his opening transaction--then market conditions and stock performance that defy expectations are probably the worst reasons for him to change that view.

Instead, he should either stay in his contract to see if the stock eventually rebounds and makes the contract profitable, or sell the contract immediately, cut his losses, and look for another opportunity that makes more sense.

Trying to Hit a "Home Run" Every Time

Popular culture portrays Wall Street as a sort of heaven for adrenaline junkies, in which highly skilled traders spend their days chasing down successively bigger, sexier, and more lucrative deals. The only barriers for these imaginary gods of the stock market appear to be failing to out-trade and outperform all their friends and colleagues and thereby missing out on bragging rights at the local pub at the end of the trading day.

A skilled options trader can make huge gains using well-planned strategies. Certainly, this should be a goal for every options trader, but it is a difficult goal to achieve for many reasons. First, the perfect storm of daily skyrocketing corporate share prices hardly ever occurs. Most stocks maintain stability and change very little from day to day, so the record conditions for a highly profitable options contract are hard to come by. As a result, if your approach to options trading strategies consists of trying to arrange contracts that guarantee payouts that are not likely to occur, or to approach market analysis from a perspective that a lesser degree of volatility is the exception rather than the rule, you will be missing the considerable opportunities the options trading market presents for disciplined investors.

Markets and indexes may not make dramatic swings very often, and that's probably a good thing. However, markets do consistently move by several points in both directions each day. By studying market behavior, you will have a better grasp of what types of changes are likely to occur and when. Using this knowledge to buy and sell options contracts that conform to sound market fundamentals can help you earn steady weekly returns. Practiced correctly, a well-disciplined approach to options trading can provide any skilled investor with the opportunity to create a source of steady residual income to enhance an existing portfolio.

Investing in Illiquid Options

The last time you prepared your company's balance sheet, filed your taxes, or studied your investment portfolio, you may have considered your "liquid assets" as part of the calculation of your total assets. Your liquid assets are those assets—such as cars and trucks, office equipment, or real estate—that can quickly be converted into cash by selling them. Assets that have value may not be considered liquid unless you can sell them for cash quickly. Selling assets for cash quickly requires a market, whether you have a garage sale, sell at an auction, or advertise in the media; but it also requires a large enough number of potential buyers that you will not have to wait for the right buyer to come along to pay you the asking price. The more buyers, the more competition, and the greater number of opportunities to make a sale, hence the liquidity of the asset. Obviously, if you are selling an obscure or unique item, regardless of its value, it will be inherently less liquid.

Like assets and stocks, illiquid options contracts have a relatively small market of buyers and sellers competing for their purchase and sale. All stock traders buy and sell the same stock for any given company; whereas a single stock can give rise to countless options contracts, each with different strike prices and expiration dates. As a result, options are more likely to become illiquid than stocks.

CHAPTER 3:

The Risks of Not Investing

Many people are thinking about investment "risk." But few take the risk of NOT spending. We need to understand both sides of the risk coin. Looking at the investment risk, we look at the potential price, and as people, we are scared of losing.

If we look at an investment's "dropping out," we look at the cost of foregone profits, which is also called a loss. "I wish I traded in Bitcoin when it was..." is a lack in psychology.

There is more to the threat of not engaging in blockchain, though, as it is not just a way to' make money,' it is a new technological step.

There have been many people back in the day who have decided not to participate in learning new technology, and there may always be.

There were people in the 80s and 90s who decided not to get interested in learning about technology, people who were late on the internet because, as one of my brother's claimed, "It is a fad that will not last."

How Much Does It Cost, Not to Learn New Technology?

How many jobs can one do in this world without having any computer skill level? No, one does not have to be excellent in skill level, but usually, there has to be a skill level to at least enter some information, even if working in a supermarket register. I opted not to do a series in workplace training when I was 13 when we started to touch type in the first term. Okay, about 3 million words ago on the internet, maybe I would save some time and add 6 million if I did not just use three fingers and my nose to write.

The risk of not spending moves beyond its immediate economics passes through most points into job opportunities, comfort, stress levels, and overall quality of life as global adoption grows. Thanks to the social acceptance of technological advances, most people have been forced to learn how to do things like bank and pay electronic payments, how to use money, how to write, how to use a computer, how to set up a firewall, how to use cloud services and how to do other things that are of a technical nature-and they have PAID for it without any hope of ROI like that.

In the not-so-distant future, the planet will be forced to learn and use the same things we are doing here because they need to be interested in the changing economy. Of course, you can argue that, but if you discuss it here on my blog, it means you have studied technology that did not exist a decade or two ago. You probably did not see most of it at the time as an acquisition phase-it was a natural progression of your existence.

Understand Market Basics

In the modern world, investment has been made accessible to the average person. Most employers who offer retirement savings plans often sponsor an education day, so employees can gain some familiarity with the types of retirement plans and options that are available to them. Also, with the proliferation of cable news networks, specialized programming, the internet, and social media, there is no shortage of information widely available to virtually anyone, anywhere.

Especially in today's information age, knowledge is power. Before you jump right into trading on the options market, take some time to familiarize yourself with the basics of market dynamics. Options traders use a language that is unique to their niche in the investment world, and many outsiders may be completely perplexed and unable to understand much of what they say. Besides, the ability to tolerate a certain amount of financial risk is an integral component of successful investing.

CHAPTER 4:

How to Start Swing Trading?

Step One: Select an Asset

The initial step of swing trading using choices is choosing an underlying advantage to trade exactly where you have identified a trading chance. Swing traders will frequently check many asset marketplaces to experience a much better possibility of locating a great setup for a trade.

When choosing an asset, search for an advantage sector due for a correction as based on a momentum signal, like the RSI, for instance. This specific signal is a bounded oscillator, which indicates that a marketplace is overbought when its value is above seventy or even oversold when its value is under thirty.

When you wish a lot more reliable swing trading signals from the RSI, you can hold back until you notice a thing known as price RSI divergence happens, which suggests the cost tends to make an additional intense in a move, like hitting a brand new high, but the RSI isn't able to achieve that. That's a lot better swing trading signal which the industry is thanks, for an imminent correction.

Step Two: Choose A Direction

Once you have determined a marketplace and used the preferred form of industry analysis, whether specialized or essential, to locate a trading chance with an excellent risk/reward ratio of two or over to one, then you definitely may feel at ease taking a directional industry perspective on the underlying asset utilizing call or put choices.

For instance, in case you believe that the industry will climb, you will utilize a call option to visit long, the basic promotion you want to exchange with restricted downside danger and limitless upside potential.

Conversely, in case the view of yours was that industry was going to fall; then, you'd rather purchase a put option to visit short the underlying asset, once again with minimal downside danger along with limitless upside potential.

The possibility payoff profiles below proven for expiration for night call and place positions shows how your losses are restricted to the premium paid in case the directional view of yours seems to be incorrect. Additionally, likely income on an alternative job is limitless and begin to accrue beyond the breakeven point in which the profits on the placement go over the premium paid.

Step Three: Pick A Strike Price

The strike cost of an alternative can help decide the price of its. Generally, the more appealing the strike cost of an alternative is a family member to the prevailing market cost for the underlying asset, the greater that alternative will set you back. Furthermore, the longer an alternative of a certain hit price has until expiration, the costlier it'll be.

When an option's strike price is right at the prevailing marketplace, it's in cash or maybe ATM, and once at a level worsen the prevailing market, it's from the cash, or maybe OTM. Both OTM and ATM choices don't have any intrinsic value.

Many swing traders want to profit from fairly short-term directional moves in a sector; therefore, they'll most likely select a relatively OTM choice that they plan will go ITM somewhat rapidly so they can sell it too. This is since choices have time value and intrinsic worth, and time great decays progressively swiftly as time advances toward expiration. It encourages a swing trader to wish to market again whatever choice they purchase at the very first chance when a respectable revenue presents itself.

Step Four: Choose an Expiration Date

Choosing an expiration date will reflect just how long you feel it is going to take for the underlying industry to achieve the objective of yours. You'll typically choose a shorter-term option in case you think the move is going to be quick or a longer-term option if you think it'll take some time.

On the flip side, you might not need to buy an alternative by having an expiration date far down the road due to the relatively high price.

Numerous swing traders are going to choose about one-month choices or maybe choices on the near futures contract, so long as it's much more than one month away because that will often allow them to have time for their view to pan out before expiration.

Step Five: Time Your Entry

Trade entry timing is normally completed using technical analysis. Since swing traders trade each fashion with corrections to those trends, they initially have to determine the prevailing trend in the asset they're looking at.

When trading with the direction, swing traders will search for a remedial pullback to create a place in the direction of the pattern.

Step Six: Execute the Trade of Yours

When the time to trade has come, it is time to perform based on the trading plan of yours. For instance, you can purchase a relatively OTM call choice in case the general trend is higher, or maybe an OTM put the choice in case the industry is trending downward.

It is likewise essential to keep in mind that the way you trade is equally as vital as in which you trade, to ensure you choose the proper broker as the trading partner of yours. Transaction costs, such as dealing fees and spreads, could accumulate over time in case you often trade as a swing trader.

Step Seven: Manage the Position

Once you have carried out a trade and also have a place, you run the danger of loss, because you bought an alternative, the risk of yours is going to be confined to the high quality you settled for. You'll additionally have to view the underlying market and control the possibility of trade appropriately.

In case you buy an OTM choice, you can try to sell it once the underlying marketplace reaches the strike price to ensure it gets ATM. This will even lead to the option of picking up additional premiums as the time value increases.

Competing with prospective profits would be a time decay, which happens for every complete day a choice gets closer to the expiration date of its. This implies that you will want to market back the choice position in the earliest available chance to stay away from having an industry according to a perspective that was directionally audio lose money due to too much time decay.

In case the industry is still like the trade of yours is going to pan out ultimately, though the temporary go you are looking to cash in on didn't materialize, you may think about giving it more hours to come to fruition.

You can accomplish this by performing a calendar spread or even roll out a trade, which entails selling again the near-term alternative you have and also buy a longer-term choice of the identical hit selling price. This stops you from taking losses as a result of the sharply improving time decay near the cash choices as the expiration approaches of theirs.

CHAPTER 5:

How to Maximize Profits

Learn to Select the Right Options to Trade

Brokerage firms can profit for being the option purchaser or perhaps an options writer. Options enable for a future benefit at both turbulent periods, even if the market is calm or less turbulent. That is important as the values of assets such as securities, currency, and resources are still changing, so no matter whatever the market dynamics are, there will be an options plan that will reap the benefits of it.

Agreements of options and plans to utilize them have described profiles of benefits and risks to explain what profit you are stood to gain or risk. The best you will benefit by offering an offer is the value of the received fee, although there are also infinite negative potentials. If you buy the options, the reward will be limitless, and then only you will risk the premium options rate.

An investor stands to benefit from any variety of market environments from bear and bull to volatile markets, based on an options approach employed. Spreads in options appear to limit all future profits and losses.

Options Profitability Basics

A call option holder aims to earn a profit if, let's say, a portfolio, the underlying commodity falls above strike price till expiry. If the price slips below strike price until the maturity, a put option holder receives a profit. The precise amount of benefit relies on the gap at maturity or when the choice role is closed between the purchase price and the right to strike price.

When the stock remains below the strike price, a call options writer works to make a profit. The trader revenue after writing the put options, if the price remains above the price of the strike. The productivity of an alternative writer is restricted to the fee they earn for writing the alternative (which is the expense of the purchaser contract). Options writers are also termed sellers of options.

Options Writing vs. Buying

When the options exchange plays out, an option holder will earn a significant refund on the investment. That is how a purchase price will go far higher than the strike point.

If the options exchange is competitive, an option writer can produce a comparatively low gain. That's because the return of the writer, no matter how much the stock moves, is limited to the premium. Why, then, write options? Since the odds are usually disproportionately on the writer side of the choice. A study by the CME (Chicago

Mercantile Exchange) in the late 1990 decade found that just over 75 percent of all expiry options had expired worthlessly.

This analysis removes choice positions that were closed or exercised before expiry. Even so, there had been three that are now OTM (out of money) per each option contract that's ITM (in the money) at expiry and thus useless is a relatively relevant fact.

Risk Resilience Calculation

Here's an easy check to measure your risk appetite and decide whether you're a stronger choice buyer or not. Let's say that you may write or buy ten agreements for call options, with every call price at 0.50 dollars. Typically, each contract has 100 shares as its fundamental asset, so ten agreements would cost 500 dollars ($0.50 x 10 x 100 agreements).

If people buy ten agreements for the call option, you are paying $500, and that's the max loss you could even incur. Your future benefit, however, is potential without limit. What's the deal, then? The probability that the exchange is successful is not very strong. Since this chance depends on the call option's expected uncertainty and the period left to expire, let 's assume 25 percent.

In the other side, if you compose ten contracts for call options, your overall advantage is the premium income number, or $500, whereas your risk is potentially infinite. The odds of options trading being cost-effective, even so, are really in your spite at 75%.

So, will you stake $500, knowing you've got a 75% possibility of losing the capital and a 25% possibility of making money? Or will you like to make a max of $500, as you have a 75 percent chance of having the whole or part of it, but got 25 percent possibility of a losing trade?

The response to these questions should give you an indication of your risk appetite and whether you're best off becoming a buyer or a writer of choices.

It's vital to know that those were the overall stats that apply to any and all options, but on sometimes, being an options writer or a purchaser in a particular item is more advantageous. Implementing the right approach at the right moment could dramatically alter those changes.

Options Strategies Reward / Risk

Although calls and puts could be merged to shape complex options trading strategies in varying forms, let 's analyze the benefit/risk of the four most simple methods.

Call Buying

It's the simplest strategic alternative. It is a fairly low-risk option because the overall cost to purchase the call is limited to the price charged whilst the ultimate profit is theoretically unlimited. While the chances of the trade becoming quite lucrative, as mentioned earlier, are usually relatively small. "small risk" presumes that a very tiny portion of the trader's capital represents the total expense of the option. Risking all resources on a sole call option will make it a very dangerous deal, and once the options expired useless, all the money will be lost.

Put Buying

it's another approach of lowish risk; however, if the exchange plays out, the possible large profit. Short selling of the underlying value is a suitable option for the highly risky strategy of buying puts. Puts may also be bought in a fund to mitigate the downside risk. But since equity indexes usually move higher across time, implying stocks appear to arise more frequently than they fall on average, the put buyer's risk / reward profile is marginally less attractive than a call investor.

Call Writing

Writing Put is a favorite tactic among experienced options traders because, in the utmost situation, the offer is allocated to the put's writer (they will purchase the product), whereas the best-case outcome is that writer keeps the entire sum of the options premium. The greatest danger of placing writing is that if it ultimately fails, the writer could end up charging more than stock. Put writing's risk / reward profile is more unpleasant than putting or calling buying, as the max reward is equal to the dividend received. However, the max loss is much greater. That said, as mentioned earlier, the chance of producing a return is greater.

Put Writing

This comes in 2 ways, veiled and uncovered, to label prose. Call Covered writing is yet another liked strategy for zero to hero options traders and is usually used to create additional portfolio income.

This includes composing requests for inventories kept in the fund. Uncovered or bare call writing is the sole domain of risk-tolerant, professional options traders because it has a close risk profile to a short stock deal. In call writing the overall incentive is proportional to the premium earned.

The greatest risk with such a covered call approach is to "called aside" the fundamental stock. With bare calls writing, the max loss is, in theory, unlimited, just as with a short sell.

Spread Strategy Options

Many traders or buyers use a spread tactic to merge stocks, purchasing more stocks to offer one or two separate options. Spreading would then mitigate the premium charged, as the option premium sold would then net against the bought premium option. In fact, a spread 's cost and return curves will limit the possible benefit or failure.

Spreads could be aimed at taking advantage of almost any expected price movements, ranging from basic to advanced. Just like individual shares, one may either sell or buy every spread approach.

Options Trading Reasons

Traders and investors conduct options trading to protect positions available (for instance, purchasing puts to protect a large position, or purchasing calls to mitigate a small position) and to gamble on possible market fluctuations of a commodity.

The greatest advantage of allowing the use of options is control. For instance, say an investment company has $900 to make use of a specific business and wants the most profit. In the relatively short term, the investor will be bullish at ABC Inc. So, say ABC trades at $100. The investor may buy a limit of 10 ABC stock. But ABC still has 3-month calls eligible for a discount of $3 for a strike cost of $100. Now the trader purchases 3 call option agreements rather than buying shares. The acquisition of 3 call options costs 900 dollars (3 agreements x hundred shares x 3 dollars).

Shortly until the call options ended, assume that ABC trades at $103 as well as the calls traded at $8, and at that time, the investor tries to sell the calls. In any scenario, here's how the return on that investment stakes up.

Buying ABC stock directly at $90: benefit = $13 each share x 10 stock = $130 = 14.4 percent gain ($130/$900).

Revenue = $8 x 100 x 3 agreements = $2,400 to premium payment of $900 = $1500 = 166.7 percent return ($1,500/$900).

The downside of purchasing the calls instead of the bonds, of course, being that if ABC had not sold over $95 by the termination period, the calls might have expired useless, and all $900 would've been lost. In reality, ABC had to exchange for the exchange only to break-even at $98 ($95 strike value + $3 premium charged), or around 9 percent higher than its price when it bought the calls. If the broker's expense to position the sale is still applied to the calculation, the product will have to sell much higher to remain competitive.

Such possibilities presume the trader was kept until expiry. With United States choices, that isn't needed. The trader may have offered the right to lock into a profit at any point until expiration. Or, if it seemed like the stock wouldn't be going past the strike point, they might offer the right for the residual time value to minimize the risk. The broker, for example, charged $3 for the options, so if time passes on, if the market price stays just below the strike price, such options could drop to $1. The trader was able to sell 3 agreements for $1, getting back $300 from the initial $900 and ignoring a loss.

Right Options Trading Selection

These are a few specific recommendations that will aid you in determining what kinds of trading options.

Expiry and Strike Price

You would be confident purchasing OTM calls because you are flagrantly bullish on CBA. Suppose you don't want to invest over

$0.50 for every call option and pay extra for 2-month calls with just a $49 strike price accessible for $0.50, or 3-month calls with just a $50 strike price accessible for $0.47. You opt to go for the above since you agree that the higher percentage strike price would be more than balanced by the expiry month.

Even if you're only mildly optimistic at CBA, and its associated 45 percent turnover was three times that of the market overall? In this scenario, you might recommend writing short-term puts to catch premium profits, instead of purchasing calls like in the earlier example.

CHAPTER 6:

Technical Analysis

No matter the kind of vehicle you choose for your actions, there are some basics that you have to be familiar with. This fundamental knowledge is mostly connected to the behavior of the markets.

If you learn how to recognize the way they behave, you will be able to anticipate the movement of the prices more accurately, thus make smarter decisions while trading. It can be interesting to note that regardless of the value that is traded on the market, some concepts can always apply to the prices and their way of performance on the market.

This can be explained by independent traders and investors being responsible for short-term price fluctuations. We can say that the price depends on the actions of the people who invest or trade values on the market and that prices react in a similar way when they are given similar input or stimuli.

The study that is dedicated to researching the ways of price behavior is called technical analysis and understanding its basic is one of the most essential education points that you will need to be able to make correct financial decisions on the market.

The Basics of Technical Analysis

Technical analysis represents a huge topic. If you decide to enter the market and become an investor, there is a high possibility that you will catch yourself coming back to studying and learning something new many times for as long as you intend to work as a trader. That is why every person knowledgeable in options trading would advise that a basic understanding of technical analysis is a very important step for every person involved in the market. However, you don't need to know everything about it right away. Since it is a large area of research, it is ok if for some aspects of your business you just research parts of the technical analysis that you are particularly interested in for that concrete project. For instance, the technical analysis offers more than a hundred indicators for analyzing the market. In reality, traders usually use three or four, mostly the most popular ones or just those that they were familiar within the first place.

If you don't limit yourself only to option trading but you do trade in general, you will realize that technical analysis can be applied to any financial instruments such as futures or stocks for example.

Technical Analysis' Foundation

The main basis of the technical analysis is found in the term known as '' market action''. Market action represents a whole personal knowledge about the trading market, and it doesn't include information that you might obtain from an insider. It can be simply defined as a study that determines: "the way that the price moves over time". If possible, it also examines its volumes and how they change over time too.

Still, the fundamental concept of technical analysis is based on the premise that the behavior of the market is a reflection of everything that happened and will happen with the price at a certain moment. Many things can have an impact on the price, and the amount of the impact depends on the market in which the trade is made. That's where technical analysis comes in, it cuts across all of those possibilities and states that all the things that can be known about the price are basically already included in the price that we see at the moment we want to trade.

This means that you shouldn't worry too much about the things that influence the price, as according to this it is enough to follow how the price changes over time and you will get all your answers. At first, many people wondered if this kind of principle can work because it sounded rather easy. If you had any doubts, the answer was already proven and it says that yes, technical analysis is successful although this kind of definition doesn't seem that complicated.

However, there is one very important aspect of this. Technical analysis doesn't guarantee the behavior of the price. It can tell you that the price will increase or decrease for a certain period, but that doesn't necessarily happen. It may or it may not. The reason for this is that regardless of the calculation that the market has to do something, it is impossible to be 100 percent sure that it will. The market has its own ways and eventually does what it wants. So, what technical analysis does is that it gives you the indication that shows what will be the most probable outcome, which means that the only certainty that you get is to know if the law of probability is on your side or not.

You can do a large number of average trades and hopefully make some profit, but you should never invest an amount of money or some valuable goods such as your house or your car if you can't afford to lose it. It is not recommended especially if one successful trade makes you confident that just one is enough to be a good technical indicator for certain gain. This is one of the reasons why the first task of technical analysis is to improve your chance for success by analyzing the prices and the way they behave on the market.

The second reason for the analysis is the fact that prices almost always change using certain trends. For instance, if the price increases its trend will be to rise until there is something that disables it from further growth. In comparison, we can say that prices act like Newton's motion law, which says that: "a body in motion will stay in motion unless acted upon by an external force." Of course, to prove this to be true, it has to happen over time. If this wasn't the case the price charts represented in many analyses wouldn't be the way they are. They would be illustrated as a random movement of the prices. The third reason is that technical analysis supposes that history will, as always, repeat itself. If certain situations happened in the past, and you see them happening once again in the present than it is highly expected that the same thing will happen in the future too. Since people are not expected to change in this equation, the second logical conclusion would be that their results will be the same too. In a nutshell- this was a very foundation of technical analysis. Don't forget that one of the most efficient ways to become good in trading and to increase your chance to become a successful investor is to be able to use most of the things that this analysis can give you.

There are a few arguments that you can hear against the use of technical analysis. Still, the only proof that you really need is the fact that this analysis works and that at least it can improve your chances to get more percentages while trading. However, we will point out some of the attitudes toward technical analysis:

One of the traders said: ''Charts only show what has happened in the past, how they can reveal what hasn't happened yet?'' The answer to this is quite simple, there is evidence from earlier trades and those pieces of evidence are used in technical analysis with the premise that history will repeat itself. This way you can anticipate at least with some fair certainty what will then happen with the price on the market. In comparison, it works in a similar way as the weather forecast, if they say that it will rain on the TV, you know that it might not rain even though they said it will, but you take your umbrella with you anyway. The same principle applies with the technical analysis and that is how you can predict the future by using the past events.

Another trader noted: "If the prices already incorporate everything there is to know, then any change in price can only come from new information that we don't know yet." This kind of idea doesn't only appear in trading options, it is present in all financial markets. It surfaces in many areas and even academics are still discussing it. Differently, from the opinion that is popular between the traders, this concept doesn't actually say that the price that is currently on the market is the correct one. It just states that it isn't possible to establish if that current price is too low or too high. That is why the smartest choice to deal with this concept is to prove in which way technical analysis really works. In the end, if everyone supported this kind of idea then we would have zero analysis and the price would be always the same. We can imply that technical analysis has self-fulfilling characteristics.

This means that if the majority of traders do the analysis and estimate that the price has to increase all of them would become buyers on the market, which would mean an increase in demand, thus price that went up. The same principle applies to the price that is supposed to go down. This is one more example in which technical analysis showed that it works. Of course, there can always be some doubts, but does it really matter to prove why the price went in the direction that you thought it would? Additionally, if a large number of traders who are not well educated and they just want to make quick profit fail, it can be seen as a sort of evidence that the idea of having a massive amount of traders regardless of their knowledge and dedication is somehow wrong from the beginning.

CHAPTER 7:

Market Strategies

Why Use Stock Market Strategies?

Here is a good question. Why is it worth using stock market strategies? You need to know that the financial instruments you are trading on, such as CFDs (contracts for difference), are already designed to be simplified and accessible for investment.

Even the platforms where you will find yourself performing from a practical point of view, your trading operations are very intuitive and can, therefore, be exploited both by industry experts who demand the possibility of trading professionally, via beginners who may never have put to this kind of tools but still want to create a monthly income by investing in the stock market.

One of the right reasons why it is worth learning the stock market strategies lies in the fact that we are sure that you too have always dreamed of finding a job that would not force you to move for long stretches, perhaps remaining stuck in traffic and city chaos, a job that does not oblige you to say yes to the boss on duty who may not even deserve to occupy that place, a job where you should not be forced to work overtime to be able to reach the end of the month charging you with stress and fatigue.

This is why we believe that trading with stock market strategies is the best possible alternative, not only offline but also online. Being independent in this promising world guarantees you the possibility to shake off the problems linked to the crisis to earn your freedom, even before the money, to become the master of your own life.

A Thousand Good Reasons to Trade with The Right Strategy

If you find yourself somehow, you have heard about the possibility of trading on the stock exchange, and maybe you know there is no way to do it online. If you want to take this path, we ask you not to feel intimidated or frightened by your possible future as a financial operator.

The stock exchange trading online has become a beginner or beginner's measure that it is. If, until today, you have only played lowly professions and do not have a higher degree, perhaps you think that you are not up to this kind of activity.

Perhaps you believe that the Stock Exchange and Markets, as well as the strategies to earn money, are beyond your means! Enough of this loser mentality.

The truth is that you are second to none, and you have the potential to be on a par with others and, why not, also to excel, especially in a world where meritocracy reigns like that of the stock market and financial markets on the internet.

Millions of people around the world have chosen the path of investment of their online capital, albeit very small. Now you can do it yourself by putting into practice the stock market strategies that we will propose to you during this guide.

Apply the Right Bag Techniques

Do you think that all these people know every single nation and all the secrets of the financial markets to be able to earn a salary at the end of the month in this kind of activity?

This is not the case. Anyone who makes money from online trading does so from little to useful knowledge. It is, therefore, not a question of quantity; it is only a question of quality.

Few but good stock market strategies will allow you to become an established and successful trader who can afford to buy whatever he wants, in total independence, and without having to ask anyone for anything.

It is necessary to know as well as to apply the right bag technique. Learn it first through theory, then put it into practice in the field of trading, testing it continuously and optimizing it based on your trading methodology.

Do not miss the topics to come and immediately discover the best stock exchange strategies, the path that will lead you to become a real trader may be extended and tortuous, but in the end it will be worth it, and you will finally feel satisfied in an occupation free from conditioning and the harassment of the world of work as it has always known it.

If you start trading today, your old life will already be in the past, because you're about to be immersed in a virtuous circle of real opportunities to become an ace of stock trading. Cheers!

Difference Between Tactics and Stock Market Strategies

Modern stock exchange strategies have been devised to permanently change the old canons of traditional investment that made everything too slow and stiff, too challenging to apply, and this caused traders many problems and dissatisfactions, so much that many were eventually led to abandon this promising activity.

With the new strategies, the goal has been to make trading affordable and feasible for everyone, the doors are wide open, and anyone who wants it today can enter without suffering the typical problems of the past.

What it takes to make the most of the strategies that we propose to you in all respects is only basic knowledge of the subject of trading. Consequently, you are not called to know everything to start earning.

Therefore, trading does not mean having a degree in economics. After all, those who would be prepared today to face 5 years of studies to earn money, it is really too much time and too much sacrifice to put in place, so the techniques that you have to use to earn are simple but effective strategies that guarantee the success of the trades in most cases.

Since in stock trading, we talk about strategies and not tactics, the former is much more successful and secure than the latter. The speech is very simple, and we want to clarify it with the following short definitions:

Investment Strategies

The strategy is the description of a long-term action plan used to set and subsequently coordinate all the actions that serve to achieve a particular, specific purpose. Strategies can be applied in all fields to reach the goal.

They, therefore, carry out the task of obtaining greater security by making a series of separate operations that help to reach an end goal. In the case of trading, we are talking about profit, which is undoubtedly the only primary aim that drives people to enter this business.

The simple tactic, on the other hand, is a course of action adopted according to the achievement of specific objectives, but in this case, we speak of small achievements in the short-term.

Adopting tactics would not be effective or satisfactory in the field of trading because it is not a structured plan, but simple plans to achieve small temporary objectives. In short, with a tactic you can also win a battle, but not war; winning a war requires a broader STRATEGY.

What all traders aim to achieve is a constant and lasting success over time that gives total security of a monthly income and specific collections on an annual basis. In stock exchange trading, it is possible to achieve all this by using strategies. Without strategies, you might perish as a trader very soon.

Applying stock exchange strategies requires attention and many precautions, especially at the beginning, when you are not much of an expert. In certain situations, when the markets become uncertain or careless, you do not know how to act, and you risk making mistakes.

At specific errors, however, the strategies cannot be remedied; in those cases, it will be the experience to act as a master and to suggest the right moves to make.

How Much Do You Earn If You Use the Best Strategy to Invest?

With financial instruments available today, profit margins are simply impressive; operating in the right way, you can earn a lot of money even on a daily basis, but at that point, you have to take into account other factors such as the skill of the trader, the ability to avoid the losses, the amount of capital you have available, but also the small strokes of luck that from time to time can help to increase profits.

The amount of money that can be earned then also depends, above all, on the financial product you intend to use. There are not very marked differences but still tangible, depending on whether you prefer to trade forex, CFD, or investing in social trading.

Stock Market Strategies and Money Management

If you intend to trade on the stock exchange, there is no doubt that you will eventually have to come into contact with the rules of money management or all that concerns the management of money and your precious investment capital.

Money Management shows you the way to correct money management, so it is fundamental in trading, but its rules are also applied in other fields that are as varied as in the domestic or business economy. Ultimately, the rules it dictates are quite simple and due to pure and simple common sense, but in any case, it will be necessary to observe them religiously to avoid running into severe problems in your career as a trader.

The creators of the first money management techniques had a clear idea that it was necessary to produce a new awareness of the use of money in their investments, for the first time imposing the concept of diversification and differentiation of the investment portfolio to reduce the risks of trading and losses on investment capital drastically.

A strategic approach to stock exchange trading cannot, therefore, ignore the knowledge of the fundamental precepts of money management that require you to always establish the spending limit and the budget available at the beginning.

In the field of trading, this will mean establishing the risks that you are willing to run within certain limits that not even an "Indiana Jones" of trading could ever think of crossing; otherwise, it would face economic suicide at the speed of light!

The principles of money management help you put both the risks and the potential profits on the scales to understand if a particular movement on the markets should be exploited or not; in other words, it helps you to know if the game is worth the candle.

If you learn to put the rules of money management into practice, your long-term success can be practically assured, but even the short and medium-term will be more probable and easily accessible. In short, all this talk turns to a need for investment efficiency.

The best traders are those who can minimize losses, which not even the guru of the economy could ever avoid and increase profits more and more.

The key to all this is precisely the fact that before learning to earn aspiring traders, the importance of learning to lose should be taught! Suffering losses and spilling money is a natural thing in trading, and you have to try to understand it and not give too much weight when a loss occurs.

The main rule of money management states that you should never, never, ever put at risk more than 5% of the total capital available in single trading operation.

CHAPTER 8

Advanced Strategies

Iron Butterfly Strategy

Iron Butterfly represents another very complex strategy. Iron Butterfly combines limited profit and risk to protect the investment. This time, you are hoping to hit a specific share price to maximize profits, but the trade can also be setup with a directional bias one way or the other. In the case of an iron butterfly, we modify the iron condor by selling put and call options at the same strike price.

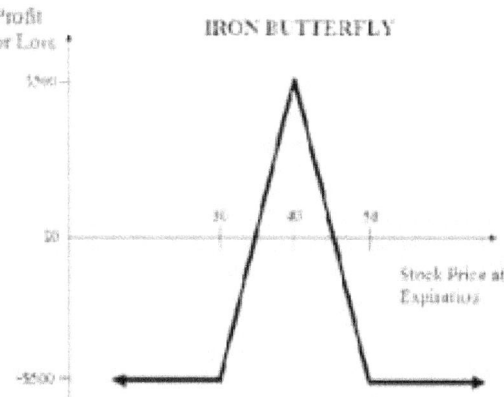

When it comes to risky strategies, one classic example is the one known as "Naked Calls." With this highly risky method investor has the possibility of writing Call Options using the underlying security of that option without actual ownership on it. The risk is high because the person who purchases that option can exercise it in which case the investor (in this case, a person who wrote the Call Option) must purchase stock to meet the order, and it has to be bought by the current market price. If this scenario happens, the risk is unlimited because it is impossible to predict the price of that stock on the market.

Strangle or The Long Strategy

One in which the investor has the opportunity to buy Call Option and Put Option together. In most of the cases, both types that the trader purchases are "out of the money," and both options must have the same date of expiration and connection to the same stock. The difference is that their strike prices aren't the same. Many people consider this strategy if they are not sure if their stock is going to increase or decrease in value.

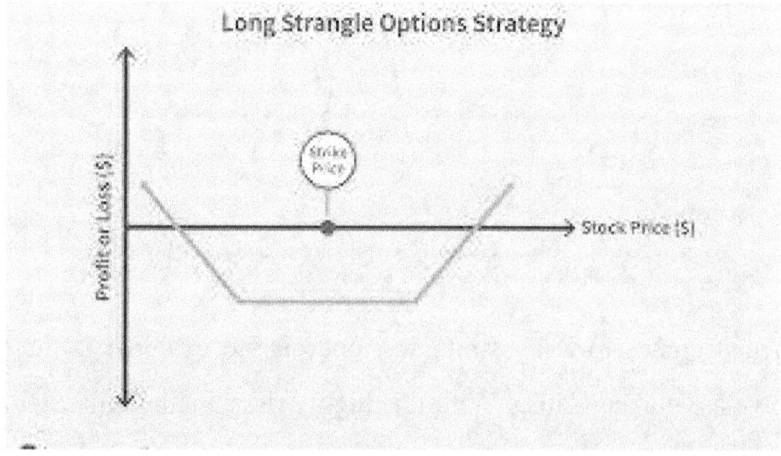

Spread Strategy

A spread is another strategy from the simple group, and it involves two types of transactions. These transactions are simultaneously executed under the normal conditions of the trade. Some experts say that spreads represent a bit advanced strategy comparing to the others mentioned above. However, for someone who is just starting, the simplest the methods the better are the results. Spreads, as our subsequent studied strategy (we will talk more about it in some of the following explanations), has a common type that is widely used. These spreads are known as vertical spreads.

Vertical spreads mean that two options, in comparison, have different strike prices. When it comes to spreading transactions, each one has named a leg, and it comes with a benefit that is one of the main reasons why investors love using spread as their main strategy. One of the best features of spread is the fact that investor's risk of the potential loss of premiums and investment in total is reduced to a minimum. However, this means that the profit that one can gain is limited too, which is why this is considered to be one of the main disadvantages of the spreads.

There are several kinds of vertical spreads. One of them is called a Bull Call Spread, and it is a spread that is mostly used by those who are considered to be bullish purchasers. This means that the purchaser would get stock and a Call Option on it for a strike price that is placed at the current market, and at the same time, he would

70

sell a Call Option on this same stock that he has but for a higher strike price. In this case, both options in trade would have the same date of expiration.

Bear Put Spread

Another kind of vertical spread that we meet often is the one called Bear Put Spread. In this strategy, the investor obtains Put Options rather than Call Options, also at the strike price that is currently on the market, and he simultaneously sells the same amount of Put Options but for a strike price that is significantly lower than the original one. The condition is that all Puts have to be connected to the same underlying stock that has the investor, and they must have the same date of expiration. Bearish investors most frequently use this type of strategy as a substitute for short selling their stocks because they es timated that the value of the stock would go down.

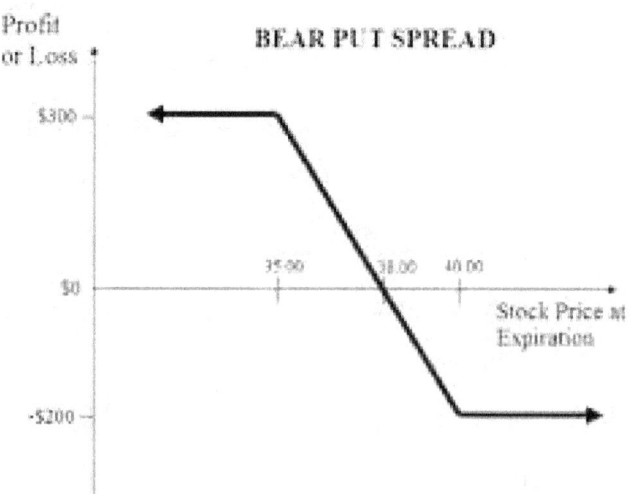

71

A few more spread strategies can appear while trading. One of them is Bear Put Spread, which also belongs to vertical spreads. Bear Put Spread is used for buying Put Options for the current strike price, and as before, at the same time, sell the same amount of Put Options for the strike price that is lower than the original one. It is, in fact, the same as with the Call Options in terms of being connected to the same underlying stock and the same expiration date. This strategy is mostly used as a substitute for short-selling stocks if the option holder predicts that the price of its stock is going to go lower.

Butterfly Spread

This strategy is more complicated than the other ones and it is not recommended for those who are inexperienced in trading. The reason for this is the fact that the option holder has to combine more simple strategies, or in this particular case, bear and bull spread.

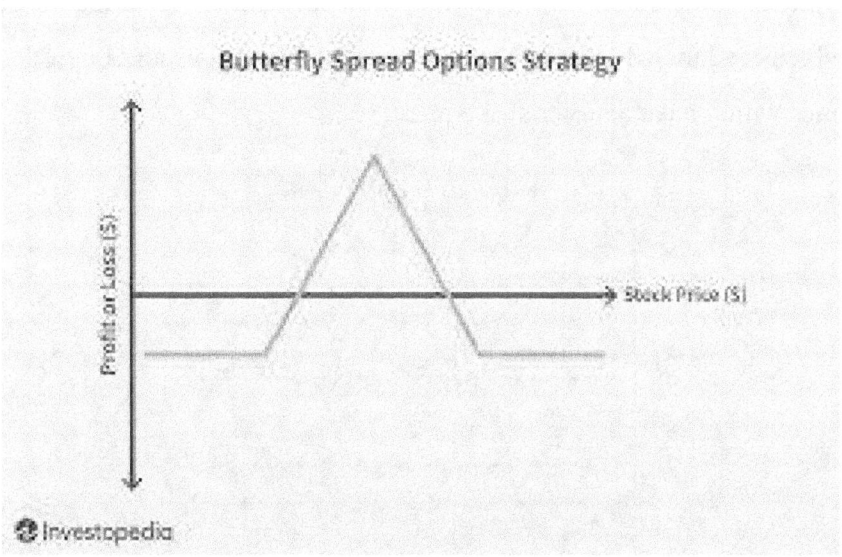

The main characteristic of this strategy is that it uses three strike prices, and all of them are different, which is why beginners shouldn't consider this method until they are confident in their skills. However, it is useful to be familiar with more complex strategies, which is why we will relearn some of them too, and far along, give some concrete examples.

Iron Condor

One of the most complex strategies for option trading is called Iron Condor. It combines short and long positions that an investor has to obtain and hold simultaneously by using two distinct strangle methods. Iron Condor enables the investor to sell Put Options that are labeled as "out of the money" and to buy other Put Options labeled the same way but at a different lower strike price. Furthermore, the investor can sell not only Put Options but Call Options too, and it works at the same principle of selling those which are labeled as "out of the money" Call Options and buy other ones which have a larger strike price.

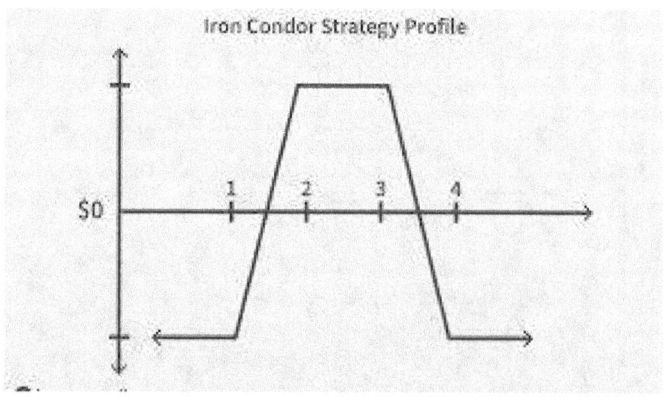

This strategy is very useful for people who want to limit the risk of their investments and have a high probability of making a profit even though it usually isn't very big. Many strategies can be used depending on the goals you want to achieve or the level of the skill that you have. Still, it is significant that you know which strategy is useful regardless of your choice of observing just marketing outlook or focusing on specific security when considering the method. We will list strategies based on this outlook. As you will see, they are also categorized as neutral ones, bull strategies, bear market strategies, exit strategies, and so forth.

Exit Strategies

Having an exit strategy is a vital part of any successful investment. You must develop this strategy before you begin options trading. This way, you will avoid losses that can are unnecessary. An exit strategy can be used at any point in time as long as it is within the time frame of the duration of the option. It means that once the expiration date has passed, you close your position or exit it anymore. Having the right timing to exit the contract is the key to either make money or lose it.

<u>Closeout Your Option</u>

One of the methods you can use as an exit strategy is to close out your option. You can do that in two ways: you can sell the option that you bought earlier, or you can buy the option that you sold before. This means that you just need to reverse your position. In case the premium for the

option has increased in the meantime, you will gain profit. However, if the premium value is lower at the moment, you would want to sell the option, and that way avoids the potential loss of the money.

When you are a writer of options, most of the time, you don't need to meet the requirement of buying the underlying security. The reason for this is the fact that you are not able even to close your position unless the option is being exercised. Even in this kind of situation, good timing is a decisive factor. We can say that timing is the single most important factor in options trading, which is why you must always carefully track your investment and estimate the right time to sell or buy options to cut losses or take deserved profits.

The volatilities of the options become more intense as the date of expiration approaches, which is why you need to keep a close eye on them.

Rolling Out

Another exit strategy that you might take into consideration is known as Rolling Out. In case you are not willing to close your position on the options, there is another solution- you can roll them. This strategy combines closing and opening positions. First of all, you need to close out the existing position and then to open new ones. Keep in mind that these newly opened positions have to be identical to the ones you have sold. The only difference is that they should have a different strike price and new expiration date (in an ideal scenario, you should have both, but more frequently, traders can obtain only one of these two things).

Exercising Options

If you don't like the concept of the previous two exit strategies, there is another one. Exercising options is a method that is used by holders that want to buy the underlying security, and they estimate that there will be a need for exercising. The only reasonable moment in which a holder chooses to use this strategy is when his or her options are "in the money" because if the options are labeled as the other two categories, it would be senseless to do so. When it comes to option writers, they don't have any control over the buyer's decision to exercise the option or not.

76

When you analyze all scenarios that can happen while trading and you decide what exit strategy will best suit you, you have to keep monitoring your position at any moment, and you have to be persistent in following through the goals that you have set and the strategies that you decided to use to make that happen. Trading options come at a fast pace, and it is easy for the person to get caught up in the short-term gain and lose the goals that were set long-term. One of the unwritten rules in any trade is that you mustn't allow your emotion to overpower you. You need to stick to the plan you have prepared because you have put time, knowledge, effort, and money into making the best possible path to make a profit with long-term goals in mind.

CHAPTER 9:

CHAPTER 9:

Trader Psychology

We associate trading psychology to some behaviors and emotions that are often the triggers for catalysts for decisions. The most common emotions that every trader will come across are fear and greed.

Fear

At any given time, fear represents one of the worst kinds of emotions that you can have. Check-in your newspaper one day, and you read about a steep selloff, and the following thing is trying to rack your brain about what to do following even if it isn't the right action at that time.

Many investors think that they know what will happen in the following few days, which makes them have a lot of confidence in the outcome of the trade.

This leads to investors getting into the trade at a level that is too high or too low, which in turn makes them react emotionally.

As the trader puts a lot of hope on the single trade, the level of fear tends to increase, and hesitation and caution kick in.

Fear is part of every trader, but skilled traders have the capacity to manage the fear. There are various types of fears that you will experience, let us look at a few of them:

The Fear to Lose

Have you ever entered a trade and all you could think about is losing? The fear of losing makes it hard for you to execute the perfect strategy or enter or exit a strategy at the right time.

As a trader, you know that you need to make timely decisions when the strategy signals you to take one. When fear guides you, your level of confidence drops, and you don't have the ability to execute the strategy the right way, at the right time. When a strategy fails, you lose trust in your abilities as well as strategy.

When you lose trust in many of the strategies, you end up with analysis paralysis, whereby you don't have the capacity to pull the trigger on any decision that you make. Making a move becomes a huge challenge.

When you cannot pull the trigger, all you can think about is staying away from the pain of losing, while you need to move towards gains.

No trader likes to lose, but it is a fact that even the best traders will make losses once in a while. The key is for them to make more profitable trades that allow them to stay in the game.

When you worry too much, you end up being distracted from your execution process, and instead, you focus on the results. To reduce the fear of trading, you need to accept losses. The probability of losing or making a profit is 50/50, and you need to accept this fact and accept a trade, whether it is a sell or a buy signal.

The Fear of a Positive Trend Going Negative (and Vice Versa)

Many traders choose to go for quick profits and then leave the losses to run down. Many traders want to convince themselves that they have made some money for the day, so they tend to go for a quick profit so that they have the winning feeling. So, what should you do instead? You need to stick with the trend. When you notice a trend is starting, it is good to stay with the trend until you have a signal that the trend is about to reverse. It is only then that you exit this position. To understand this concept, you need to consider the history of the market. History is good at pointing out that times change, and trends can go either way. Remember that no one knows the exact time the trend will start or end; all you need to do is wait upon the signal.

The Fear of Missing Out

For every trade, you have people that doubt the capacity of the trade to go through. After you place the trade, you will be faced with many skeptics that will doubt the whole procedure and leave you wondering whether to exit the strategy or not.

This fear is also characterized by greed – because you aren't working on the premise of making a successful trade rather the fact that the security is rising without you having a piece of the pie.

This fear is usually based on information that there is a trend that you missed that you would have capitalized on.

This fear has a downside – you will forget about any potential risk associated with the trade and instead think that you have the capacity to make a profit because other people benefited from the action.

Fear of Being Wrong

Many traders put too much emphasis on being right that they forget that this is a business they should run the right way. They also forget that being successful is all about knowing the trend and how it affects their engagement.

When you follow the best timing strategy, you create many positive results over a certain period of time.

The uncanny desire to focus on always being right instead of focusing on making money is a great part of your ego; and to stay on the right path, you need to trade without your ego for once.

If you accommodate a perfectionist mentality when you get into trades, you will be after failure because you will experience a lot of losses as well. Perfectionists don't take losses the right way, and this translates into fear.

Ways to Overcome Fear in Trading

As you can see, it is obvious that fear can lead to losses. So, how can you avoid this fear and become successful?

Learn

You need to find a way to get knowledge so that you have the basis for making decisions. When you know all there is to know about options, you know what to buy and when to sell, and learn which ones to watch. You are then more comfortable making the right decisions.

Envision the Bigger Picture

You always need to evaluate your choices at all times and see what you have gained or lost so far for taking some steps. Understanding the mistakes, you made gives you guidance to make better decisions in the future.

Start Small

Many traders that subscribe to fear have lost a lot before. They put a lot of funds on the line and ended up losing, which in turn made them fear to place other trades. Begin with small sums so that you don't risk too much to put fear in you. Once you get more confident, you can invest larger sums so that you enjoy more profit.

Use the Right Strategy

Having the right trading strategy makes it easy to execute your trades successfully. Make sure you look at various options trading strategies so that you know which one is ideal for your situation and skills.

Many strategies can help you succeed, but others might leave you confused. If you have a strategy that doesn't give you the returns you desire, then adjust it to suit your needs over time. Refine it till you are comfortable with its performance.

Go Simple

When you have a strategy that is simple and straightforward, you will be less likely to lose confidence along the way because you know what to expect.

Additionally, the easier the strategy, the faster it will be to spot any issues.

Don't Hesitate

At times you have to jump into the fray even if you aren't so comfortable with the way it works. Once you begin taking steps, you will learn more about the trade.

However, you need always to be prepared when taking any trade. The more prepared you are, the easier it will be for you to run successful trades.

Don't Give Up

Things might not always go as you expect them to do. Remember that mistakes are there to give you lessons that will make you a better trader. When you lose, take time to identify the mistake you made and then correct it, then try again.

Greed

This refers to a selfish desire to get more money than you need from a trade. When the desire to get more than you can usually make takes over your decision-making process, you are looking at failure.

Greed is seen to be more detrimental than fear. Yes, fear can make you lose trades, but the good thing is that you get to preserve your capital. On the other hand, greed places you in a situation where you spend your capital faster than you return it. It pushes you to act when you shouldn't be acting at all.

The Danger of Being Greedy

When you are greedy, you end up acting irrationally. Irrational trading behavior can be overtrading, overleveraging, holding onto trades for too long, or chasing different markets.

The more greed you have, the more foolish you act. If you reach a point at which greed takes over from common sense, then you are overdoing it.

When you are greedy, you also end up risking way much more than you can handle, and you end up with a loss. You also have unrealistic expectations from the market, which makes it seem as if you are after just money and nothing else.

When you are greedy, you also start trading prematurely without any knowledge of the options trading market.

When you are too greedy, your judgment is clouded, and you won't think about any negative consequences that might result when you make certain decisions.

Many traders that were too greedy ended up giving up after making this mistake in the initial trading phase.

How to Overcome Greed

Like any other endeavor in trading, you need a lot of effort to overcome greed. It might not be easy because we are talking about human emotions here, but it is possible.

First, you have to know that every call you make won't be the right one at all times. There are times when you won't make the right move, and you will end up losing money. At times you will miss the perfect strategy altogether, and you won't move a step ahead.

Secondly, you have to agree that the market is way bigger than you. When you do this, you will accept and make mistakes in the process.

Hope

Hope is what keeps a trading expectation alive when it has reached reversal. Hope is usually factored in the mind of a trader that has placed a huge amount on a trade. Many traders also go for hope when they wish to recoup past losses. These traders are always hopeful that the following trade will be the best, and they end up placing more than they should on the trade.

This type of emotion is dangerous because the market doesn't care at all about your hopes and will take your money.

Regret

This is the feeling of disappointment or sadness over a trade that has been done, especially when it has resulted in a loss.

Focusing too much on missing trade makes the trader not to move forward. After you learn the lessons after such a loss, you need to understand the mistakes you made then move ahead.

When you decide to let regret to rule your thinking, you start chasing markets with the hopes that you will end up making money on a position by doubling the entrance price.

CHAPTER 10

Trading Flexible

A successful options trader is a unique individual. This person learns how to leverage their financial position to pave a way to profitable returns that make the time and effort invested worth it. This person is strong-willed and determined.

I have tried to break down the concepts as simple as possible so that anyone can do it. The truth is that though, even though everyone has the capability to understand these concepts and maybe the ability to implement these strategies, not everyone has the fortitude to stick with it until they gain the results they want – which is financial freedom. The people that do, fall into a small bracket. A strong options trader requires a unique set of skills, attitude and persona.

The Traits of a Successful Options Trader

Being Self-Disciplined

I am sure after reading this guide, you may be excited about the possibility of gaining financial freedom by using options trading. If you are willing to jump with both feet in, I applaud you. I also implore you to exercise caution and therefore, self-discipline. Do not just stop your education on options with this reading. Do more extensive research so that you can identify the best opportunities for you. Doing this will allow you to form the best strategy for your individual case and goals. Do not skip doing your homework because you are eager. Jumping the gun has led to many traders losing out. You need to rule your desires, wants and actions rather than being ruled by them.

Being Committed

A successful options trader is one that does not give up. He or she does not trade on an on-again, off-again basis. This person is committed to the cause of building their financial success in this way and persists in their effort. Remember that this is not a hobby. This is something you embrace as a business and part of your lifestyle. Go hard or go home. Options trading has no room for being tentative.

Continually Learning

The financial market is continuously evolving. It changes every single day. A successful trader needs to be able to roll with the punches and have a clear understanding of what is happening now. He or she needs to be able to make forecasts about the future as well. Continuously learning about the market also allows you to see new opportunities where amateur traders will not. One of the best ways to increase your knowledge of options is to follow the action of an experienced options trader. The point is not to copy his or her moves. Rather, it is to watch a master at work so that you can develop your own style of trading.

Being Patient

This relates to jumping the gun. You need to carefully weigh your options before you make a move while trading options. While there are risks involved in trading options, the market typically provides signs of these opportunities if a trader knows where and how to look. Control your emotions and strategize your entry into the trade market as well as your exit from trades.

Being an Effective Risk Manager

There is no guarantee when you trade options and as such, an effective options trader needs to be able to exploit his or her position to try to determine where he or she should take appropriate measures to capitalize his or her gain. Part of managing risks involves being able to diversify your portfolio so that all your eggs are not in one basket. A successful trader does not go chasing after every option that is available. Neither does he or she get stuck chasing China eggs that do not yield gain. Even though there is no guarantee that it will all work out, being able to effectively manage risks significantly lowers the chances of loss happening.

Being Able to Manage Money Effectively

The trader also needs to know how much capital should be allocated for trading. Throwing your money at all options will not lead to effective results. Actually, this is a recipe for losing money. Part of being a good money manager means that the trader needs to be good with numbers so that he or she can calculate the vega, theta, delta and gamma of their trade options, for example.

Maintaining Accurate Records

This will help with decision-making and allows you to allocate your money effectively as you will have a history of your options within easy reach. My suggestion is that you do this digitally for easy access, better storage and better organization. Digitally record keeping also allows for the use of specialized software that makes life a lot simpler than looking through hard copies when records are needed.

Being an Effective Planner

While there is a level of relying on instinct in trading options, you also need to have a plan, so you do not place random trades. You need to have direction to effectively move forward with obtaining financial freedom no matter which option you choose to do that. Having smart goals allow you to develop this plan. You also need to have a plan to cover any losses that may happen and a plan for how you can leverage the profit that you do make. Your plan needs to allow for flexibility and the great thing is that you can upgrade, downscale and change the plan completely if need be.

Being Able to Accept Losses Gracefully

The nature of the financial market is unpredictable, and every trader makes a loss at some point. Having an apt understanding of the market will minimize this loss but you also need to be able to be flexible in how you handle this so that you do not get blindsided nor do you let this weigh you down. Remember that any successful person needs to be able to find a lesson in their failure so that they come back stronger and better in the future.

Dream Big

Many people are stuck in a state of financial dependency and insecurity because they do not see themselves being any better than they are now. Therefore, they never take any actions or risks to elevate themselves

You need to be able to visualize your success to manifest it. To develop yourself into a brilliant trader, you need to be able to see yourself in the future as a successful entrepreneur who implemented a plan to gain passive income and is, therefore, able to enjoy the freedom of using your time as you see fit.

The brain has a way of manifesting action to make what it sees a reality so use that to your advantage. See yourself as a successful options trader today. Imagine the way that you would look, the way that you would feel, how you would dress and everything else that being an options trader means to you. See yourself being more than what you are today no matter your current circumstances. Do not place any limits on yourself.

The mistake that many options traders make at the beginning is that they think small. They imagine maybe making a few hundred dollars here and there to subsidize their current lifestyle. They make that the pinnacle of their success even though many options traders make hundreds of thousands and millions of dollars every day.

The people that dream so small have their own reasons, but a common reason is that they do not want to be too disappointed if things do not work out. This way of thinking is limiting and self-fulfilling. You are stopping yourself from achieving greatness and reaching your true potential with such a mindset. Instead, you have to dream big, bold dreams. It is the only thing that will keep you motivated in the tough times. You have to know that you can do this and make this a successful business no matter the odds.

I know that at the beginning, it may be tough especially when people laugh at your dreams of becoming a success. Remember that you are not doing this for them. Those people may be your friends and family and of course, this hurt. Do not allow this to demotivate you. Keep strong and remember that you are doing this for you, not them. If you need to, make it an extra motivator to prove them wrong. Give yourself the last laugh.

Visualizing allows you to have something to work towards. The vision creates a hunger within you to manifest that picture in your

93

mind into reality. It builds anticipation and creates excitement. It gives you a sense of purpose. Allow yourself to be consumed by that passion.

My belief is that every person on this planet is capable of doing great things so stop limiting yourself. Stop underestimating your potential. One of the most significant attributes of an options trader is being able to follow his or her gut. You will never develop that knack for trading options if you continually doubt yourself and your purpose.

All of the traits that are stated above are things that can be learnt. So, it is fine if you have not developed these traits as yet. The point is to make it a habit to develop them starting today. The first thing you need to do is picture yourself as the successful options trader that you will be in the future. Then put in the work to make that vision a reality.

CHAPTER 11:

Money Management

What Is Money Management?

Money management is all about how you handle your finances, your savings, your expenditure, and investments. It is making sure you can survive a financial crisis. It means planning a budget for your long-term goals and also making investments that will help you to successfully achieve your goals.

When you manage your money, you will be able to make wise purchases. Otherwise, you will always complain of having less amount of money no matter how much your income is. It can also be known as investment management.

Money management is more about risk. When you have better money management skills, you will reduce the risk. You must understand all the areas of money management to be able to avoid any risks. Plan with a negative bias, always ask yourself "what-if" scenarios, take action, and plan.

When budgeting for money management, make sure you are spending less than what you save. Excellent money management will help you monitor your spending before going beyond your budget. By doing this, you will secure your savings.

You will be able to invest if you make the right decisions. Avoiding taking on more risks will help you reach your financial goals. The strategies you use in your investments play a significant role in your success. Here are some of the basics, advantages, and disadvantages of money management:

The Advantages of Money Management

Better tracking of your money. When you have a reasonable budgeting plan, you can track how you use your money, and you can monitor every expense. This is a significant profit to you, as you can spend less and end up saving more money.

Monitor your expenses for some months and then change your budgeting by removing the less required expense and allocate that money to your savings plan, a retirement plan, or a vacation fund. Excellent money management will help you stay on track; you will be able to pay your bills on time, will be able to stay within your limit, and avoid bank account overdraws.

Poor money management can put you in bad debt quicker than the blink of an eye. You can prevent those nasty fees charges when you go over your limit. By having an excellent budgeting plan, you will avoid overspending.

A good retirement plan. Better money management and savings plans will help you in the long term. You will be able to secure your future and have an excellent retirement plan. With better money management skills will give you a better retirement plan for you. No matter how much you save, even when you save and invest a small amount of money, it will provide you with a more significant amount for your retirement.

Peace of mind. Proper money management brings you peace of mind. Having bills on the counter and having no idea on how you will pay the bills or not having the money to purchase something that you needed.

All these issues can be difficult to face each day. Managing your money wisely and experience all the profits of sound money management, you will enjoy peace of mind, and you can provide for yourself and your family, too.

The Disadvantages of Money management

Rapid changes.

With the rapid changes in the financial world, it is required to change your management plans every time. It is sometimes challenging to adjust your planning to incorporate the fast-changing situations. Unless your plan can help to adopt the new techniques, it will be limited.

Time-consuming.

Managing your money can sometimes be a time-consuming exercise. It requires you to make the estimates as accurate as possible. However, you can use software and mobile applications to assist you with planning, and this may reduce the time you will take if you were not using the technologies. And if you have less knowledge about money management, it will take you more time to achieve this.

Inaccuracy.

When planning, you make a lot of assumptions in terms of estimation of your expenses. Any shift like economic downturn or the change in the currency rate or interest rates can change your estimates in your planning.

Money Management Problems to Avoid

Research shows an increasingly growing interest in people learning about retirement and financial planning. This is excellent news; however, most people don't save enough for their retirement. About 18% are on the right track to reaching their income retirement goals and 4% average national saving rate, which is below 10-15% the recommended saving for retirement by financial planners. It is very common to encounter some problems with money management even after getting your finances together for many years. These problems can be significant and can be simple sometimes, the everyday difficulties everyone gets at one point in their lives. However, by practicing and learning, you will be able to avoid these problems in the future. The key is avoiding money management problem, to have peace of mind, and be able to save more money. Here are some of the problems that you should avoid achieving a successful financial future:

Living from paycheck to paycheck.

If you are already breaking on Sunday and you were to receive your salary on Friday, then there is a huge problem. Aim at having enough money in your bank to take care of your living expenses for the coming 3-6 months. Ideally, you will have enough money to cover 8-2 months to cover you during the hard times.

You will be required to set aside money from each paycheck and save it in the bank. You can consider having a savings account so as you can make direct deposits. By doing this, you will avoid money problems in the future when you encounter issues like loss of a job, illness, or a home renovation.

Spending more than what you need.

You probably dine out a little too often. Buying many lattes every week. Are you going to the movies a little too much? All these small things add a strain to your pocket in the long run. The small purchases add up to a high cost if you are charging them into your credit card.

You can choose other low-cost ways of achieving this–for example, carrying your lunch and coffee and minimize dining out or buying coffee every day. All these small changes will help you in the long term. Cut down on the needless expenses to avoid this money problem.

Poor investment choices.

Looking for ways to make huge money faster, like the get rich quick schemes, will only put you into more debt. To make money, you have to save money even while in debt. You can consult a credit counselor to help you plan to pay off your debt while you are saving through a smart budget.

Not having a savings plan.

You should have a budget and a saving plan, no matter your age or your level of financial knowledge. Write down your finances and save the plan. Start tracking your net income. You can use mobile applications like Personal Capital and create a saving spreadsheet. By doing this, you can know where you are overspending, which area you can save more, and be able to make better financial decisions. Creating these spreadsheets will help you improve your finances.

Having only one source of income.

One thing that can bring money problem is having only one source of income. To be able to be financially secured and successfully build a savings and retirement portfolio, you need to have more than one source of income.

101

For example, many very wealthy people have many income streams. Don't rely on the stability of the 9-5 work only because the company might do down, and you are left with no job and a source of income. You might have some savings to cover your expenses while you look for a job, but all this can be stressful. You can consider freelance work as a source of income, and you can start a blog or rental properties. Having a side hustle will help you a lot when you lose your full-time job.

Misusing your tax return money.

Many people misuse their tax return money on needless expenses and forgetting to spend that money on their debts and other emergency savings. By saving this money, you will be able to increase your savings and offer some relief to your debts. It might not be exciting, but you will be setting yourself to a more secure financial position.

Money Management Strategy

This is about responsibly managing your money and having stable finances. Maximize your savings by implementing a money management strategy. The strategies range from aggressive to passive, and it depends on your initial approach. Aggressive strategies include greater leverage and broad profit goals. And passive strategies include capital preservation. Here are some of the money management strategies you should be aware of:

Budget and adjust accordingly.

The first step in managing your finances is by creating a budget. Many people ignore budgeting because they find it hard to estimate their spending, and they have the numbers to use a starting point. It is very common for the actual numbers not to be spot on, but budgeting will help you be more mindful of your spending and what you can do to improve.

The more practical way is to know how much your income is and deduct the monthly fixed expenses. These expenses include rent, insurance, transport, and food. These expenses are constant every month, so you can easily predict them. By creating a budget, you can compare your actual numbers and the monthly or yearly expenses. You will be able to have an accurate budget with time and experience.

Save for retirement.

Have a great investment plan, but don't forget to plan for your retirement. Find retirement plans where you can charge your retirement. Talk to a financial advisor or a bank and find out your options. You can decide to set up a SIMPLE 401(k), SIMPLE IRA, SEP-IRA, or employer-sponsored 401(k) plan.

Research these plans and choose the one that meets your retirement goals. You don't need to deposit a lot of money towards your retirement account. By saving over some time, it will help you to control your tax bill and tax-defer until you start accessing your retirement.

Establish an emergency fund.

Having an emergency fund for your finances is essential to cover you during an emergency, like job loss and illness. Without an emergency fund, even small expenses like repairing a fried laptop will be impossible. You might decide to get a short-term loan to cover these expenses, but these loans carry a hefty interest rate. The short-term loan might help you to take care of the loan, but the cost will attract more cash issues in the long run.

Putting it into action, the hardest part is finding the money to create an emergency fund. From your income, find ways to cut costs or find an additional source of income to be able to make more money. Put the emergency fund in a savings account or find a money market account but do not invest the money. This way, the money will be easily accessible when you require it. Start small and grow your emergency fund over some time.

CHAPTER 12

A Project for Success

Know When to Go Off Book

While sticking to your plan, even when your emotions are telling you to ignore it, is the mark of a successful trader, this in no way means that you must blindly follow your plan 100 percent of the time. You will, without a doubt, find yourself in a situation from time to time where your plan is going to be rendered completely useless by something outside of your control. You need to be aware enough of your plan's weaknesses, as well as changing market conditions, to know when following your predetermined course of action is going to lead to failure instead of success. Knowing when the situation really is changing, versus when your emotions are trying to hold sway is something that will come with practice, but even being aware of the disparity is a huge step in the right direction.

Avoid Trades That Are Out of The Money

While there are a few strategies out there that make it a point of picking up options that are currently out of the money, you can rest assured that they are most certainly the exception, not the rule. Remember, the options market is not like the traditional stock market which means that even if you are trading options based on underlying stocks buying low and selling high is just not a viable strategy. If a call has dropped out of the money, there is generally less than a 10 percent chance that it will return to acceptable levels before it expires which means that if you purchase these types of options what you are doing is little better than gambling, and you can find ways to gamble with odds in your favor of much higher than 10 percent.

Avoid Hanging on Too Tightly to Your Starter Strategy

Your core trading strategy is one that should always be constantly evolving as the circumstances surrounding your trading habits change and evolve as well. What's more, outside of your primary strategy you are going to want to eventually create additional plans that are more specifically tailored to various market states or specific strategies that are only useful in a narrow band of situations. Remember, the more prepared you are prior to starting a day's worth of trading, the greater your overall profit level is likely to be, it is as simple as that.

Utilize the Spread

If you are not entirely risk averse, then when it comes to taking advantage of volatile trades the best thing to do is utilize a spread as a way of both safeguarding your existing investments and, at the same time, making a profit. To utilize a long spread, you are going to want to generate a call and a put, both with the same underlying asset, expiration details, and share amounts but with two very different strike prices. The call will need to have a higher strike price and will mark the upper limit of your profits and the put will have a lower strike price that will mark the lower limit of your losses. When creating a spread, it is important that you purchase both halves at the same time as doing it in fits and spurts can add extraneous variables to the formula that are difficult to adjust for properly.

Never Proceed Without Knowing the Mood of The Market

While using a personalized trading plan is always the right choice, having one doesn't change the fact that it is extremely important to consider the mood of the market before moving forward with the day's trades. First and foremost, it is important to keep in mind that the collective will of all of the traders who are currently participating in the market is just as much as a force as anything that is more concrete, including market news. In fact, even if companies release good news to various outlets and the news is not quite as good as everyone was anticipating it to be then related prices can still decrease. To get a good idea of what the current mood of the market is like, you are going to want to know the average daily numbers that are common for your market and be on the lookout for them to start dropping sharply. While a day or two of major fluctuation can be completely normal, anything longer than that is a sure sign that something is up. Additionally, you will always want to be aware of what the major players in your market are up to.

Never Get Started Without A Clear Plan for Entry and Exit

While finding your first set of entry/exit points can be difficult without experience to guide you, it is extremely important that you have them locked down prior to starting trading, even if the stakes are relatively low. Unless you are extremely lucky, starting without a clear idea of the playing field is going to do little but lose your money. If you aren't sure about what limits you should set, start with a generalized pair of points and work to fine tune it from there.

More important than setting entry and exit points, however, is using them, even when there is still the appearance of money on the table. One of the biggest hurdles that new options traders need to get over is the idea that you need to wring every last cent out of each and every successful trade. The fact of the matter is that, as long as you have a profitable trading plan, then there will always be more profitable trades in the future which means that instead of worrying about a small extra profit you should be more concerned with protecting the profit that the trade has already netted you. While you may occasionally make some extra profit ignoring this advice, odds are you will lose far more than you gain as profits peak unexpectedly and begin dropping again before you can effectively pull the trigger. If you are still having a hard time with this concept, consider this: options trading is a marathon, not a sprint, slow and steady will always win the race.

Never Double Down

When they are caught up in the heat of the moment, many new options traders will find themselves in a scenario where the best way to recoup a serious loss is to double down on the underlying stock in question at its newest, significantly lowered, price in an effort to make a profit under the assumption that things are going to turn around and then continue to do so to the point that everything is completely profitable once again. While it can be difficult to let an underlying stock that was once extremely profitable go, doubling down is rarely if ever going to be the correct decision. If you find yourself in a spot where you don't know if the trade you are about to make is actually going to be a good choice, all you need to do is ask yourself if you would make the same one if you were going into the situation blind, the answer should tell you all you need to know.

If you find yourself in a moment where doubling down seems like the right choice, you are going to need to have the strength to talk yourself back down off of that investing ledge and to cut your losses as thoroughly as possible given the current situation. The sooner you cut your losses and move on from the trade that ended poorly, the sooner you can start putting energy and investments into a trade that still has the potential to make you a profit.

Never Take Anything Personally

It is human nature to build stories around, and therefore form relationships with, all manner of inanimate objects including individual stocks or currency pairs. This is why it is perfectly natural to feel a closer connection to particular trades, and possibly even consider throwing out your plan when one of them takes an unexpected dive. Thinking about and acting on are two very different things, however, which is why being aware of these tendencies are so important to avoid them at all costs. This scenario happens just as frequently with trades moving in positive directions as it does negative, but the results are always going to be the same. Specifically, it can be extremely tempting to hang on to a given trade much longer than you might otherwise decide to simply because it is on a hot streak that shows no sign of stopping. In these instances, the better choice of action is to instead sell off half of your shares and then set a new target based on the updated information to ensure you are in a position to have your cake and eat it too.

Not Taking Your Choice of Broker Seriously

With so many things to consider, it is easy to understand why many new option traders simply settle on the first broker that they find and go about their business from there. The fact of the matter is, however, that the broker you choose is going to be a huge part of your overall trading experience which means that the importance of choosing the right one should not be discounted if you are hoping for the best experience possible.

This means that the first thing that you are going to want to do is to dig past the friendly exterior of their website and get to the meat and potatoes of what it is they truly offer. Remember, creating an eye-catching website is easy, filling it will legitimate information when you have ill intent is much more difficult.

First things first, this means looking into their history of customer service as a way of not only ensuring that they treat their customers in the right way, but also of checking to see that quality of service is where it needs to be as well.

Remember, when you make a trade every second count which mean that if you need to contact your broker for help with a trade you need to know that you are going to be speaking with a person who can solve your problem as quickly as possible.

The best way to ensure the customer service is up to snuff is to give them a call and see how long it takes for them to get back to you. If you wait more than a single business day, take your business elsewhere as if they are this disinterested in a new client, consider what the service is going to be like when they already have you right where they want you.

With that out the way, another thing you will need to consider is the fees that the broker is going to charge in exchange for their services.

There is very little regulation when it comes to these fees which means it is definitely going to pay to shop around. In addition to fees, it is important to consider any account minimums that are required as well as any fees having to do with withdrawing funds from the account.

CHAPTER 13:

Choosing the Right Strategies

When selecting an option technique, we will look at the essential factors you require to consider. When share trading, you have chance to purchase the option, then sell or hold your position. With options, there are many more options, each with various risks and chances.

No matter the method you pick, your objective will be to either earn a profit or restrict a prospective loss. In pursuit of these objectives, as a buyer of options you seek to purchase your OPTION at the most affordable price possible, and after that offer it (or exercise it) at the highest price reasonable. As an options writer, you work directly against the buyers in seeking to offer your options at the highest cost possible, and after that, close them out at the most affordable price possible or see them end useless.

For any options trade, the motion in the OPTION premium while you hold it will identify if you earn a profit or loss. You, for that reason, should think about all the elements that will trigger a modification in your OPTION premium. These aspects include: Movement in the rate of the underlying stock (and all the factors that might affect this).

Modifications in volatility.

This is share trading in contrast, where you only require considering the motion in the cost of the stock. Time decay and modifications in volatility are distinct to trading options.

Pointer.

Even if the underlying stock price is in relocations in your direction, you can still make a loss due to the impact of time decay or an unforeseen modification in volatility.

Movement in price.

The most significant factor affecting the cost of your option is motions in the cost of the underlying stock. You need the view of formed how the market cost of the underlying stock move is going. Since the time limitations in trading options, you likewise need to form a view of the cost motion of the underlying stock over a particular time duration and match your options expiration to this frame time.

You can determine your view on the movement price of the underlying stock using fundamental analysis, technical analysis, or a mix of both. The technique used to form your opinion is not appropriate to choose your options technique, as long as you can hypothesize about the movement of rate within the restricted life of an OPTION.

The following general guidelines can be used about picking an OPTIONS method based on your view of the cost motion in the underlying stock:

You might consider composing options as a method if you are expecting that the rate of the underlying stock will stay within a limited cost range. Once again, time decay, the reason for this is. If the underlying stock rate remains reasonably static, there will be little change in the intrinsic worth and a decline in time value, triggering the cost of the options to fall. The revenue capacity for an option writer is always the premium got, so big price motions in their favor are not beneficial to OPTION authors as they do not affect the revenue made.

Tip.

Option writers are typically looking for time decay to minimize the value of the options they compose so that their options expire worthlessly. The options author then keeps the option premium as a revenue.

Time decay.

All options have a minimal life that is specified by the option expiry date. All options will go through time decay over the life of the opportunity, and this reduction in time value will increase as the OPTION approaches the expiry date.

Time works against options buyers as they are speculating on a considerable cost movement in the underlying stock to happen before the expiration date. Not just do option purchasers require to hypothesize on a price motion, this motion should take place before the expiration date.

Tip.

Your view on the timing of cost movement in the underlying stock will affect your option of the expiry month.

As an OPTION purchaser choosing an expiry month, you need to balance versus having sufficient time for the stock price to relocate your favor and the cost of this time. Longer-dated options have a more significant time worth and, as a result, will likewise have a more significant premium. The OPTION strategy success will be extremely reliant upon the time that you have to the options expiration date, and the quantity you spent for that time.

As an OPTION seller, you need to stabilize the additional premium you get for longer-dated options versus the increased possibility that the underlying stock price will move against you in this time, and you will incur losses over and above your option premium.

CHAPTER 14

Trading Errors and Mistakes

Options trading is basically every trader's point of interest, and you can make handsome profits from it too. If you have come this far, then you already know the potential that this field has, but if you make the wrong trades, it can be equally devastating for your career. So, if you want to take this seriously, here are some mistakes that are commonly made, and once you know them beforehand, you will think twice before making them yourselves.

Not Having a Trading Plan

Not following any plan for trading is probably the most common mistake of all, especially among the beginners. It might be that you read in some finance magazine that a particular company's stocks are performing well, or maybe you got a tip at a random gathering, and you decided to act it. Well, should you? The answer is both yes and no. No, because you should never take anyone on their word when it comes to trading. Yes, because it might actually turn out to be a good tip in certain cases, but you first have to perform quick research of your own and then decide whether that tip would be worth believing or not.

If you do not have a trading plan before you dive into the world of options trading, it is simply as if you are driving your car, and yet you do not have a license. So, when you face a situation of crisis, the losses can be huge. In options, you do not have all the time in the world. There is a fixed amount of time within which you have to take action; otherwise, your option will expire worthless. You always have to be alert for any opportunities that might come your way, and if there is an opportunity, don't ever miss it. So, your goal of making a lot of money might not just be in your favor just because you did not make a plan for it. Remember that no matter how good your strategy is, sometimes even they can fail when you do not have a trading plan.

Some of the things that your trading plan should definitely possess are the type of options that you are particularly interested in like Nifty, equity, commodities, and so on, the amount of money that you can afford to invest in trading on a monthly basis, the amount of money you want to invest in each trade, your risk appetite, and your expected returns from a trade. Make sure that this plan is followed for every trade that you conduct. You will be getting temptations of going off the track, but you have to resist those temptations and prevent yourself from risking too much. Your fear and greed both have to be controlled if you want to make it big. If you are just a beginner, start small and then work your way up to the top slowly and steadily.

Believing in the One-Size-Fits-All Concept

Selecting the strategy that would work best for you depending upon the situation of the market is what options trading is all about. Suppose you discovered a good strategy, and you have been using it for quite some time, and it is working out well for you. But that specific strategy is not meant for all types of trades. For example, you cannot use strategies of a bullish market in a bearish tone. So, if you keep repeating your strategy without even evaluating the trades, thinking that it will work like some magic wand and make you win every trade, then you are wrong. You have to learn to predict the market outlook and then choose the strategy that is best for you.

You have to perform technical analysis and fundamental analysis to find out which strategies you should use. Both macro and microeconomic factors have to be taken into consideration. Gather knowledge from different places by reading and going to workshops. Read the views of experts from different reputed finance magazines. After you have studied the market outlook, picking the right strategy would become much easier.

Ignoring the Expiration Date

The expiration date of options is one of the major factors affecting our trades. As you know that in order to make profits, you have to speculate on the direction of the stock movement. Well, at the same time, I am also asking you to speculate how much time is it going to take a particular point because, in the case of options where your time is limited by expiration date, it cannot take you forever. Let us say that you researched and found some factors that can positively impact the price of the stock, but do you, when that price is going to reach the level you want it to reach?

Trading does not only mean looking after strategies. In the case of options, you have to look out for the expiration dates as well. Just like the strategies, when it comes to the expiration date, you have a multitude of choices for it too. But once you have built your market outlook, settling for the right expiration date kind of becomes the easy task. For example, you can ask yourself how much time you think a particular trade will need in order to play out. You can also ask yourself whether you want to hold a trade through major events or not like a stock split or a public announcement. Lastly, you should also ask yourself whether you have the required liquidity to pursue after this.

Overleveraging the Trades

It is always advised to beginners to get used to stock investment before you start options trading. When you have done stocks investing first, it is more likely for you to have handled huge amounts of money directly, and in fact, buying stocks directly also means that you have to pay the entire share price.

So, for this example, let us say that you are a person who has the capability of buying stocks worth $1000 at a time, and let's say that you have done this before but not in options. Now that you have switched over to the options because of their cheap nature and that they are a derivative. If you had to buy the underlying asset directly with all your money, it would have cost you way more money than what you're investing in purchasing the options. So, you don't need to invest a thousand dollars for purchasing that many amounts of stocks in the form of options contracts.

But this also poses a risk – a risk where you might end up overleveraging. Leverage is a powerful tool only when you use it wisely. So, just because there is leverage doesn't mean that you should invest more amount than necessary.

That is why there is a very common rule that is followed – consider it as a rule of thumb in your case. Try and limit your loss to within 5% for every trade that you do. This is something that you have to strictly abide by so that all your capital is not lost behind any particular trade. When you lose only some money in a trade, you can always pick yourself back up and invest in a different trade.

Error in Position Sizing of Your Trades

There are two common emotions that are responsible for all errors related to position sizing. These emotions are greed and fear. Suppose you are making a decision, and you become too greedy about your profits, then it might happen that you position your trade too big that it is not right for the size of the account that you have. And this is even more common when your outlook of the market is wrong and then what you get in return is not profit but a crippling loss recovering from which can become really difficult.

This was just one mistake of position sizing. The other one is when you position your trade too small. There is nothing wrong with trading small, but do you know what it means? It means that you might not get the chance to make any substantial profit at all.

Here are some common ways in which you can maintain appropriate position sizing –

- Make sure the risk percentage for each trade is somewhere around 1-5% of your total account value.

- For every trade, it is better that you stick to a consistent dollar value like $100 or $1000 based on how much you can afford to risk.

No matter what you do or which strategy you use, your position sizing should be such that you are comfortable risking that amount of money. In simpler terms, even if the trade does not happen like you predicted it to be, it won't hurt you to lose the money invested. In the ideal case, your trade value should be such that it is meaningful enough, but not too big that it has reason to make you lose your sleep at night.

Buying Options Based on Whether They Are Cheap or Not

Human beings tend to think that whenever something is cheap, it is better to buy it rather than going for something that is costly. They think that this is the most cost-effective thing to do. But what you don't understand is that with options, following this 'cheap' tactic is not going to help you. In fact, it is going to ruin your trade. It is usually said that an option tends to be more out-of-the-money when its premium is more towards the lower side. Yes, at first glance, it might appear to you that you have just found the biggest steal of your life but trust me when I say this, don't fall for the trap because even if you get it, making any money with the help of that option would be highly unlikely.

When the premiums of options are towards the lower side, the strike price of those options is usually either well below or well above the market price. In simpler words, if you had to make money with such an option, then there has to be a miraculous change in the price for you to do so. So, let us say you bought a call option that has a very low premium, but if you want to make money with it, it has to show a drastic movement upward. Similarly, there has to be a drastic movement downward if you want to make money after buying a put option with a low premium.

CHAPTER 15

Finding A Suitable Market

The Market Environment

The market is a chaotic place with a number of traders vying for dominance over one another. There are a countless number of strategies and time frames in play and at any point, it is close to impossible to determine who will emerge with the upper hand. In such an environment, how is it then possible to make any money? After all, if everything is unpredictable, how can you get your picks right?

Well, this is where thinking in terms of probabilities comes into play. While you cannot get every single bet right, as long as you get enough right and make enough money on those to offset your losses, you will make money in the long run.

It's not about getting one or two right. It's about executing the strategy with the best odds of winning over and over again and ensuring that your math works out with regards to the relationship between your win rate and average win.

So, it really comes down to finding patterns which repeat themselves over time in the markets. What causes these patterns?

Well, the other traders of course! To put it more accurately, the orders that the other traders place in the market are what creates patterns that repeat themselves over time.

The first step to understanding these patterns is to understand what trends and ranges are. Identifying them and learning to spot when they transition into one another will give you a massive leg up not only with your options trading but also with directional trading.

Trends

In theory spotting a trend is simple enough. Look left to right and if the price is headed up or down, it's a trend. Well, sometimes it is really that simple. However, for the majority of the time you have both with and counter-trend forces operating in the market. It is possible to have long counter trend reactions within a larger trend and sometimes, depending on the time frame you're in, these counter-trend reactions take up the majority of your screen space.

Trend vs Range

This is a chart of the UK100 CFD, which mimics the FTSE 100, on the four-hour time frame. Three-quarters of the chart is a downtrend and the last quarter is a wild uptrend. Using the looking left to right guideline, we'd conclude that this instrument is in a range. Is that really true though?

Just looking at that chart, you can clearly see that short-term momentum is bullish. So, if you were considering taking a trade on this, would you implement a range strategy or a trending one? This is exactly the sort of thing that catches traders up.

The key to deciphering trends is to watch for two things: counter trend participation quality and turning points. Let's tackle counter trend participation first.

Counter Trend Participation

When a new trend begins, the market experiences extremely imbalanced order flow which is tilted towards one side. There's isn't much counter trend participation against this seeming tidal wave of with trend orders. Price marches on without any opposition and experiences only a few hiccups.

As time goes on though, the with trend forces run out of steam and have to take breaks to gather themselves. This is where counter trend traders start testing the trend and trying to see how far back into the trend they can go. While it is unrealistic to expect a full reversal at this point, the quality of the correction or pushback tells us a lot about the strength distribution between the with and counter-trend forces.

Eventually, the counter-trend players manage to push so far back against the trend that a stalemate results in the market. The with and counter-trend forces are equally balanced and thus the trend comes to an end. After all, you need an imbalance for the market to tip one way or another and a balanced order flow is only going to result in a sideways market.

While all this is going on behind the scenes, the price chart is what records the push and pull between these two forces. Using the price chart, we cannot only anticipate when a trend is coming to an end but also how long it could potentially take before it does. This second factor, which helps us estimate the time it could take, is invaluable from an options perspective, especially if you're using a horizontal spread strategy.

In all cases, the greater the number of them, the greater the counter-trend participation in the market. The closer a trend is to ending, the greater the counter-trend participation. Thus, the minute you begin to see price move into a large, sideways move with an equal number of buyers and sellers in it, you can be sure that some form of redistribution is going on.

Mind you, the trend might continue or reverse. Either way, it doesn't matter. What matters is that you know the trend is weak and that now is probably not the time to be banking on trend strategies.

Starting from the left, we can see that there is close to no counter trend bars, bearish in this case, and the bulls make easy progress. Note the angle with which the bulls proceed upwards.

Then comes the first major correction and the counter-trend players push back against the last third of the bull move. Notice how strong the bearish bars are and note their character compared to the bullish bars.

The bulls recover and push the price higher at the original angle and without any bearish presence, which seems odd. This is soon explained as the bears slam price back down and for a while, it looks as if they've managed to form a V top reversal in the trend, which is an extremely rare occurrence.

The price action that follows is a more accurate reflection of the power in the market, with both bulls and bears sharing chunks of the order flow, with overall order flow in the bull's favor but only just. Price here is certainly in an uptrend but looking at the extent of the bearish pushbacks, perhaps we should be on our guard for a bearish reversal. After all order flow is looking pretty sideways at this point.

So how would we approach an options strategy with the chart in the state it is in at the extreme right? Well, for one, any strategy that requires an option beyond the near month is out of the question, given the probability of it turning. Secondly, looking at the order flow, it does seem to be following a channel, doesn't it?

While the channel isn't very clean, if you were aggressive enough, you could consider deploying a collar with the strike prices above and below this channel to take advantage of the price movement. You could also employ some moderately bullish strategies as price approaches the bottom of this channel and figuring out the extent of the bull move is easier thanks to you being able to reference the top of the channel.

As price moves in this channel, it's all well and good. Eventually though, we know that the trend has to flip. How do we know when this happens?

Turning Points

As bulls and bears struggle over who gets to control the order flow, price swings up and down. You will notice that every time price comes back into the 6427-6349 zone, the bulls seem to step in masse and repulse the bears.

This tells us that the bulls are willing to defend this level in large numbers and strongly at that. Given the number of times the bears have tested this level, we can safely assume that above this level, bullish strength is a bit weak. However, at this level, it is as if the bulls have retreated and are treating this as a sort of last resort, for the trend to be maintained. You can see where I'm going with this.

If this level were to be breached by the bears, it is a good bet that a large number of bulls will be taken out. In martial terms, the largest army of bulls has been marshaled at this level. If this force is defeated, it is unlikely that there's going to be too much resistance to the bears below this level.

This zone, in short, is a turning point. If price breaches this zone decisively, we can safely assume that the bears have moved in and control the majority if the order flow.

Turning Point Breached

The decisive turning point zone is marked by the two horizontal lines and the price touches this level twice more and is repulsed by the bulls. Notice how the last bounce before the level breaks produces an extremely weak bullish bounce and price simply caves through this. Notice the strength with which the bears break through.

The FTSE was in a longer uptrend on the weekly chart, so the bulls aren't completely done yet. However, as far as the daily timeframe is concerned, notice how price retests that same level but this time around, it acts as resistance instead of support.

For now, we can conclude that as long as the price remains below the turning point, we are bearishly biased. You can see this by looking at the angle with which bulls push back as well as, the lack of strong bearish participation on the push upwards.

This doesn't mean we go ahead and pencil in a bull move and start implementing strategies that take advantage of the upcoming bullish move. Remember, nothing is for certain in the markets. Don't change your bias or strategy until the turning point decisively breaks.

The current order flow and price action are what matters the most, so pay attention to that above all else. Also, note how the candles that test this level all have wicks on top of them.

This indicates that the bears are quite strong here and that any subsequent attack will be handled the same way until the level breaks. Do we know when the level will break? Well, we can't say with any accuracy. However, we can estimate the probability of it breaking.

The latest upswing has seen very little bearish pushback, comparatively speaking, and the push into the level is strong. Instinct would say that there's one more rejection left here. However, who knows? Until the level breaks, we stay bearish. When the level breaks, we switch to the bullish side.

Putting It All Together

So now we're ready to put all of this together into one coherent package. Your analysis should always begin with determining the current state of the market. Ranges are pretty straightforward to spot, and they occur either within big pullbacks in trends or at the end of trends.

Trends vary in strength depending on the amount of counter-trend participation they have. The way to determine counter trend participation levels is to simply look at the price bars and compare the counter-trend ones to the with trend ones. The angle with which the trend progresses is a great gauge as well, for its strength, with steeper angles being stronger.

Then, you need to determine the turning point of the trend. The turning point is a level that is extremely well defended by the with trend players and will be attacked repeatedly by the counter-trend traders in long trends.

Conclusion

By now, you must have figured out how easy options trading is. With the information covered here plus your desire to make it in options trading, you can easily excel in this business. You are now better prepared to trade options using technical analysis, fundamental analysis, and other procedures. You are also ready to take opportunities as they come and have a sense of what each trade entails, from a technical view.

By now, you understand that there are a good number of tools and platforms that you can use to trade options. Since the cost of options keeps fluctuating from the start date to the maturity date, you need a platform that best suits your trading and training needs. Bear in mind that each platform has its strengths and weaknesses; therefore, you may not find one that is 100 percent effective. A good platform is one that gives you the ability to tailor your experience. Such a platform can accommodate both novice and experienced traders. A sophisticated platform can negatively impact your proficiency since you will spend a considerable amount of time trying to understand the advanced tools and features on the platform. Having the right instrument will equip you to trade with confidence.

Of course, we could not end the discussion without mentioning financial leverage as a benefit of trading options. The leverage comes about when you are able to translate your little capital into huge gains. The more you invest, the higher the financial leverage. With a good trading plan, you can use this concept to minimize trading risks and maximize your returns. A great advantage in options trading is that the options contract itself is already a leverage opportunity. It allows you to grow your starting capital easily. By now, you should be able to calculate the leverage of any given position using the delta value.

When it comes to options trading, patience and commitment are the key. You must be able to control your emotions. Emotional trading is a risky affair. Treating options like any other business can help manage losses with ease. Making trades just because they seem good can lead you into trouble. Actually, the difference between good traders and average ones is that a good trader does not allow emotions to get the better of him. When he loses, he understands that it is because he made a wrong move or choice and that it is not the system that is working against him. Good traders do not dive into unnecessary opportunities just because of feelings; they weigh the options and make decisions based on what is in the trade for them. They also understand when to quit from trade even if some losses are incurred.

We also looked at some of the tips you need to employ to ensure that you succeed in most of your trades, if not all. These are simple things such as collecting enough capital before you start trading, identifying a suitable trading style, and having a risk management plan. You also have known some of the mistakes most traders make when trading options and how you can avoid them.

With all this insight into the options market, you should be able to carry out a trade from start to finish, successfully. You must, however, note that the options business is not for every investor. It can get sophisticated and dangerous if you do not put the information outlined in here into practice.

By now, it is clear to you whether this is an investment you want to try out or not. If you are into it, then you must decide the kind of trader you would want to be. As a day trader, you will have the advantage of making several trades that close quickly. This option is good for you if you are interested in making small profits. Otherwise, consider long-term trading that can span a period of over 30 days but with incredible profits.

Trading on options also involves choosing the underlying security that you would wish to connect your options to. This may be in the form of commodities, stock, or foreign currency. Each currency has its own characteristics, and the liquidity status also matters. Commodities are good but very volatile, currencies trade most of the time, but the prices are easily influenced by economic news items. Stocks experience a rapid change in prices overnight.

To many people, options are a complicated instrument to trade in. However, the more you learn about them, the simpler they become. With some experience, you realize that the instrument is one of the most flexible to trade in. Nonetheless, for options trading to go well, you also need to understand the basics of picking a stock, assessing market cycles and formulating investment strategies.

Since options are highly volatile, if you do not exercise caution, you may lose all your investment at one go. That is why you need specialized training such as this one before venturing into it. A good number of people who have succeeded in options trading began as stock traders. If you are already into stock trading, you will have easy time trading options due to the many similarities that exist between the two.

Lastly, it is important to note that the shorter the trading period, the higher the stress and risks involved. If you keep holding your trades through the night, you stand a high risk of losing all your capital and destroying your account. Other than this, we are glad that you have learned a new way of earning money from the financial market and understood all the traits and skills you need to make it in binary options trading. Note that theory is never effective without practice. So, in case you need to get started, it is best to identify a trading platform and put what you have learned into practice. Remember, the more you practice, the more confident you become.